PRAISE F ‖‖‖‖‖‖‖‖‖‖‖‖
T0032094

THE LANGUAGE OF LENORMAND

"A magical mélange of assorted practical teachings with hands-on exercises, *The Language of Lenormand* is a window into the passionate workings of the analytical wisdom of Erika Robinson, a marvelous Lenormand diviner. It is always a privilege to look through the eyes of an experienced diviner, let alone a Lenormand seer. Erika holds the reader's hand and walks them step-by-step, offering warm guidance sprinkled with a playful wit. You will find yourself smiling while learning the Lenormand system through fresh eyes."

—Rana George, author of *The Essential Lenormand*

"Erika Robinson's unique voice adds an edge to the information many in the Lenormand world already know, and yet may have never utilized. Where *The Language of Lenormand* really differs from other Lenormand books lies in Erika's approach in emphasizing each card's number, not just its meaning, so that reading a Grand Tableau becomes effortless. Her personal viewpoints and life experiences create a depth of narrative, allowing readers to feel comfortable in addition to creating a new perspective."

—Callie L. French, illustrator of *La Santa Muerte Lenormand*
and *Rana George Lenormand*

"Erika Robinson generously shares her joy and expertise in this exquisite Lenormand guidebook. She has cultivated an easy-to-understand and compelling method to engage with the cards, inviting us to explore and find ourselves through the 'language of pictures.' As someone who has created several Lenormand decks, I highly recommend this much-needed and beautifully expressed 'how-to' filled with personal experience, interpretations, and historical information. *The Language of Lenormand* goes far beyond teaching and inspires us to find the wonder in our lives."

—Monica Bodirsky, creator of *Shadowland Lenormand,*
Shadowland Tarot, and *Between the Worlds*

"An amazing resource for all budding Lenormand readers, *The Language of Lenormand* by Erika Robinson seamlessly breaks the Lenormand deck down into bite-sized pieces, allowing readers to consider their own understanding of the system at each step. An easy-to-read guide with a personable touch that walks the reader through the labyrinth of Lenormand meanings and into an integrated system of reading, this book adds fun to the Lenormand system and enables the reader to enjoy every step of the process. A must-have for all!"

—Toni Savory, founder of the World Divination Association
and coauthor of *The Sirens' Song*

"Erika Robinson's background as an English teacher blends perfectly with her expertise in Lenormand. She walks the reader through the cards, incorporating very well-timed divinatory techniques and exercises, so that the information sinks in effortlessly. She then integrates the next piece of information, creating a natural flow that resembles the way a language is taught. *The Language of Lenormand* is indispensable for beginners and eye-opening for seasoned Lenormand readers and teachers."

—María Alviz Hernando, director of the World Divination Association.

"Whether you're a novice seeking to unlock the oracle's mysteries or a seasoned practitioner eager to deepen your understanding of the fabulous Lenormand, *The Language of Lenormand* by Erika Robinson is an absolute must-read. With her invaluable guidance, you'll embark on a transformative quest, gaining the tools, knowledge, and confidence to navigate the intricate word language of the Lenormand with grace, wisdom, and profound insight."

—Alexandre Musruck, author of *The Art of Lenormand Reading*

"Erika Robinson uses her unique skill sets as both an English teacher and a seasoned diviner to lovingly introduce *The Language of Lenormand* from the ground up. Her pragmatic approach will have readers working with card combinations right from the first chapters in a way only a seasoned educator can accomplish. Readers will fall in love with these thirty-six cards that, when used in combinations, can uncover unlimited hidden knowledge."

—Donnaleigh de LaRose, tarot and Lenormand educator, host of the cartomancy podcast, *Beyond Worlds, Your Tarot Tribe*

THE LANGUAGE OF
LENORMAND

A Practical Guide for Everyday Divination

ERIKA ROBINSON

FOREWORD BY CARRIE PARIS

WEISER BOOKS

This edition first published in 2023 by Weiser Books, an imprint of
Red Wheel/Weiser, LLC
With offices at:
65 Parker Street, Suite 7
Newburyport, MA 01950
www.redwheelweiser.com

ISBN: 978-1-57863-805-5

Library of Congress Cataloging-in-Publication Data

Names: Robinson, Erika, 1956- author. Title: The language of Lenormand : a practical guide for everyday
divination / Erika Robinson. Description: Newburyport, MA: Weiser Books, 2023. | Summary: "The
Lenormand deck, consisting of 36 numbered and named cards, has been popular in Europe for centuries,
and has now been embraced in North America. Each card depicts an archetype a fox, a snake, a
coffin, or whip, for example - rather than tarot's somewhat more involved symbology. This makes the
Lenormand system an easy entry point to divination"-- Provided by publisher.
Identifiers: LCCN 2023024960 | ISBN 9781578638055 (trade paperback) | ISBN
9781633413061 (ebook) Subjects: LCSH: Divination. | Fortune-telling by cards. | BISAC: BODY,
MIND & SPIRIT / Divination / Tarot | BODY, MIND & SPIRIT / Divination / General
Classification: LCC BF1773 .R58 2023 | DDC 133.3--dc23/eng/20230706
LC record available at https://lccn.loc.gov/2023024960

Cover and text design by Sky Peck Design
Interior images © Red Wheel/Weiser
Typeset in Weiss

Printed in the United States of America
IBI

10 9 8 7 6 5 4 3 2 1

For Nancy Hendrickson:

That love is all there is, is all we know of love.

—EMILY DICKINSON

Table of Contents

Foreword

In the vast landscape of divination, we often find ourselves yearning for answers and seeking solace in the depths of life's mysteries. Many have turned to the Tarot, an intricate and ancient language that illuminates the hidden truths that surround us. However, mastering the complexities of the Tarot can feel like navigating an uncharted sea, requiring dedication and a great deal of study.

Luckily there is a less daunting solution and practical tool within the realm of divination—the Lenormand deck. With its thirty-six cards, a Lenormand deck offers a simpler and more accessible approach to understanding the intricacies of our lives. It is within this realm that esteemed Lenormand diviner Erika Robinson has expertly woven her knowledge into a remarkable guide known as *The Language of Lenormand*.

Erika's extensive experience as an English teacher, spanning over thirty years, has equipped her with a rare ability to distill complex concepts into a language that speaks to the hearts of learners. Her book is not just a practical guide, but also a gentle mentor, guiding readers on a transformative path toward fluency in the language of Lenormand.

With this book, Erika has created a sanctuary of knowledge and insight. Rather than presenting a mere catalog of card meanings, she delves deeper, encouraging readers to cultivate a personal connection with their deck. Erika's compassionate and thoughtful prose evokes a sense of care and guidance, igniting the reader's intuition and empowering them to explore the nuanced narrative possibilities of each card.

As a deck artist and fellow Lenormand diviner, I am intimately acquainted with the elegance and efficacy of this practical tool. In Erika's book, I have discovered a treasured resource that not only imparts wisdom, but also nurtures a profound connection to the language of this set of cards. Her writing strikes a harmonious balance between compassion and insight, offering vivid explanations of each card's significance and illuminating their interplay within easy-to-follow spreads.

Within the pages of *The Language of Lenormand*, you will uncover a wealth of meaning and guidance, all presented with a genuine spirit of friendship and support. Erika's words become a beacon of light, guiding you through the intricate web of Lenormand divination. Her caring approach encourages you to trust your own intuition, allowing the cards to speak to you in their unique and resonant voice.

The Language of Lenormand is not just a book; it is a testament to Erika's dedication and expertise, as well as her unwavering commitment to helping diviners of all levels find their own voice within their deck and build their own lexicon, making it uniquely their own. This remarkable work is an invitation to embark on a transformative journey, to uncover the wisdom that lies within the practicality of Lenormand.

Whether you are a novice, seeking to immerse yourself in the magic of Lenormand, or a seasoned diviner, eager to expand your understanding, *The Language of Lenormand* will be your steadfast companion. Allow Erika's words to enfold you within their warmth and wisdom as you explore the boundless possibilities that unfold when you communicate fluently with and through your deck.

Embrace this invaluable resource, and may it empower you to unlock the answers and insights that lie within the cards, guiding you and your sitter toward a deeper understanding of the world around you.

—Carrie Paris, creator of *The Relative Tarot* and
The Sirens' Song: Divining the Depths with Lenormand and Kipper Cards

Acknowledgments

Thank you to Sylvie Steinbach for her book, *The Secrets of the Lenormand Oracle,* the only resource in English when I began reading. Thanks to my daughter, Kiana, for being my patient first sitter. Thank you to my mother, Leola, who first taught me the comfort and the power and the wisdom of words. And thanks, as well, to the thousands of people around the world for trusting me to read for them.

Introduction

Why would you want to learn to read Lenormand? Because it is an oracle, which, if taught carefully and learned well, will remind you of the long-ago days when you delighted in paging through picture books with no words, convinced, because you understood what was happening in those drawings, that you were, in fact, reading well before you had learned your alphabet. Lenormand is a divination instrument full of archetypal images that will speak to you in ways that make you feel heard and understood. In such times as these, we can feel adrift and at odds, sometimes with others and often with ourselves. Lenormand is a road back to ourselves, to each other, to our understanding that we are never alone, but instead held, supported, guided, by a Universe just waiting for us to seek its comfort and counsel.

Many of us recall our first efforts at learning to read. For some, the process was a joy, the key that slid easily into the lock of a door we longed to open. For me, it was that way. When I was three years old, I held my mother's hand as she navigated the streets of New York City with an assurance I found perplexing. When I could contain myself no longer, I tugged at her hand, and she leaned down to see what I wanted. "How," I asked her, "do you know when to go straight and when to turn a corner? How do you know how to get us from where we are to where we want to go?" My mother smiled at me, straightened her back, and lifted her free hand to point upward, so that my gaze would follow her arm's trajectory.

"You see those cards sticking out of those poles?" she asked. "Those are street signs. There are letters on them that make words. I look at the words and they tell me which way to turn, or if I should go straight. When you learn how to read, you will be able to know when and where and how to go anywhere you want."

This, I thought, was magic.

I took to reading quickly, and teaching others to read and to write would become my life's work. I learned my craft first by sitting in my mother's lap, listening to stories she read me, with her hand guiding my own along each letter of each word as she spoke it. My mother taught me to write my letters and to sing the alphabet song so that I knew the order the letters came in, and then she taught me that if I changed around the order of those letters, I could make any word at all. *Dog* could become *God* with a simple change of letter order. Words and sentences could convey information, shift perspective, evoke strong emotion, and then, stem that emotion too. It struck me as a wonderful way to make sense of myself and of the world around me.

Learning Lenormand was like that for me: a word language spoken through pictures. I want it to feel like that for you. I want you to learn its rules, yes, but only so that you can make those rules work for you, bending them when bending is called for and shaping the language of Lenormand into what feels lyrical and lovely, natural and native, to you as the unique reader you are.

Craft is generally understood to be something handed down, explained, modeled, practiced, and honed. Activities long thought to be the provenance of women, such as cooking, sewing, weaving, knitting, tend to be labeled as *craft*. In a patriarchal world, the turn of phrase used is generally not *labeled as*, but rather *relegated to*, insuring a tacit understanding of *craft* as inferior to *art*. Art, we are to understand, implies a degree of refinement, a lighter touch, an endowed giftedness not widely considered inherent in craft. As I teach you how to read Lenormand, I would like to shift this perspective a bit, but with the following caveat:

Craft, I believe, has the capacity to ground, to steady, to establish order. It is the necessary launchpad from which art may then catapult itself into being. To read and to write, one must learn letters, which requires rote memorization. One must be taught to hold a pen by having one's hand guided by another hand that is surer, wiser, more practiced, often older. It is only through repetition—and perhaps some biting of the lower lip and maybe the shedding of a frustrated tear or two—that one learns the craft of drawing letters and stringing those letters together in ways that can erect castles or move mountains out of the way. You know what they say about gain requiring pain. No adage comes from nowhere, and the mastery of craft is hard work. Reading and writing are no exceptions.

You may already know this. For you, maybe learning to read was no fairy-dusted, alchemical wonder, no easy turning of a key in a lock. It could be that your cramped hand became slick with sweat as you gripped your pencil in a vain struggle to achieve proper penmanship. Perhaps you stuttered with every syllable of every word you tried to sound out; maybe words swam before your eyes, sneakily switching places on the page in ways that left you dizzy, tongue-tied, and confused and your parent or teacher impatient and annoyed. Probably what followed from that was shame, and maybe even the conviction that this reading and writing business was something you were "just not good at." If anything approximating that experience was yours, I am sorry. I wish I could have been your teacher and saved you from some of that angst.

If you are someone like me, who found joy in reading from the beginning of your relationship with words, my goal is to recreate for you that initial frisson of delight at such a discovery every time you reach for your Lenormand deck. If you are someone whose first encounters with reading were fraught and distressing, my goal is to teach you to read in a new way with the Lenormand cards—one whose only goal is to cause you to feel empowered, creative, and supported, just as you did when you leafed through large picture books with no words in them at all.

Before any one of us could read words, we were able to understand pictures. Pictures, as one might say in the vernacular, "just hit us different." Lenormand is the word language of pictures, as oxymoronic as that may sound. My intention is for this book to make you both craftsperson and artist: to teach you the craft of Lenormand divination first; to allow you to read in a way that feels natural and comfortable using the system's rules. But then, I do not want you to remain rule-bound, as seems to be the temptation for many Lenormand readers. As the Blake quote I began with notes, "He who binds to himself a joy / does the winged life destroy." To stay singularly bound by the rules of any system, in any context, is to cut off the possibility for creative, intuitive insight. As Blake continues, "But he who kisses the joy as it flies / lives in eternity's sunrise." I want to show you how the rules are both the launchpad and the landing site for any reading, but I also want to show you the in-between: a sacred, soaring space in which neither rules nor ego play any part.

The first time I prepared to do a professional reading in a bona fide metaphysical shop, I found myself incredibly nervous. I had set up my reading space in a way my mother would have described as "mystical-magical." The lighting was low, the candle lit, the crystals artfully arranged. My first walk-in client would be announced at any moment. I thought to myself, "Erika, what if this sitter poses their question, you pull the cards, and your mind goes completely blank? What if you have to say to your sitter, 'Beats the hell out of me . . . What do *you* see?'"

As soon as I had that thought, I burst out laughing. I knew that would never, ever happen. I had read hundreds of people at that point, most of them via phone, email, or anonymous Facebook post. People from a world away would ask me questions like:

What does he think of her?

In the very beginning, I would wonder, "Who is *he?* And what about *her?* Is this a father and daughter, brother and sister, boss and employee, love interest? How in the world am I supposed to answer a question like that with no context at all?"

Then I remembered that the Greeks have two word for time: *chronos* and *kairos*. Chronos is the time with which we are all familiar: the time as found on a watch, a clock, a calendar. It is the measure of our days, our years, our lives. Kairos, on the other hand, can enfold and encompass chronos, but it is so much more. When I was small and asked my mother a question to which she did not either know the answer or want to share it, she would give me a long look and say, "You'll know in the fullness of time." Even as a child, I knew that meant, "Not today, and not anytime soon." That fullness of time—that's kairos.

Once a Lenormand diviner has learned the rules of the craft and is willing to take Blake's unbounded leap by "kiss[ing] joy as it flies," that diviner must be willing to put their ego in their car's back seat with a juice box, an iPad, and instructions not to kick the back of the diviner's seat. Such diviners are then equipped to get behind the wheel and embark on a journey from chronos—their everyday, quotidian home—to kairos—the land where the past, present, and future all simultaneously reside, where our Higher Selves sit companionably with the Universe to observe our comings and goings. The Lenormand diviner who takes this journey forms a pact with their sitter to access that sitter's kairos-kept vault, to extract from the sitter's Higher Self the answers to their questions. Only then does the diviner return to the familiar realm of chronos, carefully cradling what they have collected. Only then does the diviner translate for the sitter, using Lenormand, the language that sits *between* chronos and kairos.

The point is, we are never unguided when we read, so long as we leave the ego out of the equation. The ego is too chronos-bound for such an elevated endeavor as translating the language of the heavens into the language of the earth.

Still, diviners and sitters—earthbound though we may be—are certainly all made from the stuff of stars. And so, that first day reading in a shop, I reminded myself that as a diviner, I am vessel, conduit, and walker between chronos and kairos. I reminded myself that my work is to deliver messages, but also to make sure my sitter knows that such work would be impossible without their participation and permission. I am a diviner and a teacher who has no interest in withholding anything of any sort from those I teach or read for. I do not wish to be perceived to be in some superior space. That is ego. I want the art and the craft of Lenormand to be disseminated as widely as possible, because to work with Lenormand is to feel both the lightness and the heft of the gifts of agency, autonomy, responsibility for growing in compassion for others and for self. The world certainly could use more of that from all of us.

My intention for this book is for it to help you see Lenormand as part of what Toni Morrison called a giant tool box; for you to see your hand as guided by the Universe to choose the right instruments (the cards) to listen for and then to craft into spoken words messages that are helpful, healing, and resonant; messages that adequately address what Morrison so aptly describes as the world's "chaos, confusion, disorder." My goal is for the work of Lenormand Divining to feel as all the best work should: like sacred play. You will know yourself as both craftsperson and artist, and you will come to see art and craft as two sides of a whole, as you are equipped with an instrument that can help bring wholeness to yourself and to others.

FIRST THINGS

Lenormand is a divination system that traditionally consists of thirty-six picture cards. Above all, it is a word language. Its thirty-six pictures, strung together in myriad combinations, become sentence, then paragraph, then story. And from the hand and mouth of a gifted diviner, such a story becomes allegory, caveat, and comfort.

Here is an example:

Think of the word *dog*. In your mind's eye, you have a vague image of a four-legged animal with a snout and a tail—your basic, generic dog, right? Now, I want you to think about a fluffy, white dog, a toy poodle, its tail wagging so hard the whole back half of its body is in motion as it sticks its little, insistent tongue out seeking to lick you into a fit of laughter so hard that it makes your stomach hurt. You see what I did there? I took the word *dog* and made it *come alive* for you by stringing other words in front of and behind it.

Think of the word *dog* again: that amorphous four-legged, snouted, and tailed animal. Now, allow that dog to become a huge, shiny, black doberman, straining at the chain holding it back from ripping out your throat, which you know it wants to do from the wild look in its bloodshot, bulging eyes, its sharp fangs visible in its gaping mouth, which drips in salivating anticipation.

How did that little foray into fear feel for you? How did I take you from "Aww! How cute!" to "Ohh! Get me out of here!"? By taking that same word *dog* and surrounding it with other words, I could paint for you a very different picture from the first one. This is the power of pictures, especially the archetypal pictures in a Lenormand deck: they evoke emotional responses to which the Lenormand diviner gives resonance through paying attention, watching with a third eye and listening with a third ear, so that the cards and second sight and second sound can be translated into language that makes a sitter feel known, heard, and understood—not just by the diviner, but also by the Divine.

Again, when you learned to read as a child, you learned individual letters, and then learned to put them together to form words, as in *d* and *o* and *g* mean *dog*. You learned that a *d* is just a *d* until it is given the company of other letters. Lenormand is like that. Each card has several discrete meanings, but no single card functions by itself. Unlike Tarot, where a reading can be given with a single card, Lenormand is a divinatory instrument meant to function collectively, preferably in groups of three or more cards together. When those of us who are boomers learned to read, one of our first sentences was "See Spot run." But before we could see Spot run, we agonized over the *s* and the *e* and then the next *e*. By the time we got to the *n* in *run*, it was kind of hard to care about who Spot was and what he was doing. Fortunately, though, all of you exploring this book can read, so you get to skip the bitter, medicinal, sounding-out part and go right for the dessert: sight-reading whole sentences with pictures. Lenormand actually does have its own *dog*—Card 18. We will get to it in time, and you will welcome it as an old friend, but there are other cards whose acquaintance you will make first.

I will be teaching you the thirty-six traditional Lenormand cards in order, and in groups of three, which will allow you to begin sight-reading immediately. When we have learned three groups of three cards, I will show you how nine cards together are just like the "Nine Ladies Dancing" in the "Twelve Days of Christmas" song you may well have heard a time or two. You will have learned a lot about the craft of Lenormand at that point, and as we make our way through the next trio, and then next, you will see what Robert Frost means in his poem "The Road Not Taken," when he reminds us of how "way leads on to way." This is what we call *scaffolding* in teacher-education speak. Your confidence with the cards will grow, and you'll come closer and closer to understanding the joy of Lenormand, while at the same time, you will feel an eagerness to test the boundaries of the craft and artistically expand into Blake's "joy as it flies" by letting your intuition and your Higher Self show you not just the chronos abilities of Lenormand, but its capacity to catapult you to kairos, where the juiciest, richest, and most soulful messages reside.

You will have thirty-six cards, your compassion, and your intuition tucked into Morrison's "giant tool box," and you will be able to use your artistry to craft readings whose message—should your sitters be ringed around the world waiting for a reading one at a time each time you divine with your cards—would speak specifically and intimately to each of them alone. And in your own quiet times of despair or questioning, of joy or anticipation, the tool box will be available always to you as well.

As a Lenormand diviner, you will have at the ready a navigational instrument that can be as blunt or as delicate as you the diviner are yourself. If you treat it with respect, Lenormand will be a stalwart, truth-teller type of friend, and one that you never have to worry that you are waking from sleep or boring with triviality. My goal is for you to feel the same wonder I feel every time I pick up the cards at the fact that in its wisdom, the Universe has made it so that mere ink on cardboard can show us the way home to each other and ourselves.

CHAPTER 1

Rider (1) / Clover (2) / Ship (3)

Rider

1

CARD 1: RIDER

(News, Message, Imminent Incoming Information)

Usually portrayed as a person on horseback carrying something in their hand, the most important thing to notice about the Rider (1) is neither the person nor the horse, but rather, what they come to convey. As I have mentioned before, Lenormand cards are not meant to be read individually, but rather to be parsed together with their sisters. Therefore, when we see the Rider (1) we must not succumb to the altogether human instinct to immediately ascribe a value to the message the Rider (1) carries. The card itself tells us nothing about whether the message carries news that is good, bad, or something in between. Sometimes—actually, most often, in Lenormand—a card is just a card, until its sisters tell us more. So for now, let this just be a horse with someone on its back, who carries some news for us in their hand.

Clover

2

CARD 2: CLOVER

(Luck, Lightness, Nature, Allergies, Fast, Fun, Surprise, Short-Lived, Quick-Acting, Unserious)

Of course, all of us recognize clover when we see it. In the Western world, anyway, we are quick to link to clover the idea of luck, serendipity, the color green, the month of March, St. Patrick's Day, and perhaps parades and all manner of merriment. It is understandable and fair that we make those associations, but in Lenormand, Clover (2) stands for more than just these associations. Right off, with Card 2, you will begin to grasp the art that must be married to the craft if Lenormand is to be read well: when the Clover (2) appears, how are you to know whether it refers to fun or to fast? To nature or to a nut allergy? The short answer is the one I have already given you: no card is accurately read in isolation. Each Lenormand card acts as a member of a collective: they help each other along by each contributing what they have to offer to create a common language.

I call Clover (2) one of Lenormand's "happiness cards," of which there are three, and all of them are floral in nature. The word *happiness* itself is a little bit generic, again, as all words are, until joined to other words. That is how all Western language functions. Clover (2) implies a kind of giddy happiness—a Santa's-reindeer-hoofs-on-the-roof happiness, a happiness for which you hope you have your camera handy, because it is ephemeral, fleeting, here and gone. But with Clover (2), we are not meant to focus on the fading. We are meant to live in Clover (2)'s moment joyfully, in the present, without thought to what came before or to what might come after.

Clover (2)'s a pretty Zen kind of card, I think. It's about the here and now. And all of that is well and good, but what if you have a sitter who comes to you with questions of love? Say they are going on a blind date that evening, and they ask you if this new person will be "the one." Say you are a diviner of some age and experience, and your sitter is young and sweet and eager. I had a sitter like this with a question like that. I pulled the cards, and Clover (2) was prominently placed in a way that caused me to sit back and take a breath before I began to read. I asked my smiling sitter where she was planning to meet this blind date, and she said, "At his hotel."

"At the bar?" I asked, trying to look innocent myself. "Or in the restaurant?"

"No," the girl replied. "He gave me a room number."

I stared at the cards a long moment, wanting to convey what I saw in a way my sitter would hear me. I talked about what Clover (2) and her sister cards were showing me: that the date would probably be fun, but perhaps of shorter duration than my sitter expected. I showed her how the cards suggested she meet this person at the bar or the hotel restaurant, so that she would at least get a drink and a meal out of the evening. Together with the other accompanying cards, the Clover (2) showed me that, to answer my sitter's question, this person was not going to be "the one"—a good time was what he had in mind, full stop. I assured her that if that was fine with her too, then a good time would indeed be had. But if her hope was that this good time would lead to love and marriage and children and a long and happy life together, the cards showed that none of that was on offer. Remember that not all of this information came from the Clover (2) card alone, but together with its sisters, the message came through clearly, and my sitter, though disappointed, was grateful. Knowledge is power, right? The next week, this sitter returned to tell me she had not bothered to show up for the date at all. I suspect that may have been just as well, particularly as my sitter was looking for a soulmate and not a one-night stand.

Ship

3

CARD 3: SHIP

(Travel, A Relocation or House Move, Overseas, Foreign, Progress)

Sometimes in the language of Lenormand a ship is just a ship. But sometimes, it is a plane, train, automobile, bicycle, motorcycle, or even one's own two feet. It is a card that bespeaks forward motion of any sort, really. Exactly what sort, as always, would be informed and dictated by the surrounding sister cards.

• • •

So now you have learned the first three cards along with their disparate and discrete meanings. Rather than move on now to Cards 4–36 and making you memorize meanings the way you were forced to deal with boring lists of sixth grade vocabulary words, I think it's time for us to take our first three cards out for a spin. Let's see how they can join hands and dance. You will notice throughout this book that, whenever I make mention of a card, I attach its number. Think of this language as you might French, where the article *le* or *la* precedes every singular noun always. The Lenormand numbers are as important as these French articles. Eventually, you will even be able to read a spread with just the numbers alone, which I did when I traveled to Asia once without a deck. I simply took pieces of paper, labeled them one through thirty-six, and voilà! I had a Lenormand deck to read with! Learning the numbers as part of each card will come in handy when we get to a more advanced technique later on. For now, trust me. When you think *Rider*, think 1. When you think *Clover*, think 2. When you think *Ship*, think 3. You will thank me later.

1. Rider (1) / Clover (2) / Ship (3) = News (Rider 1) will come in that will delight and surprise (Clover 2) about a trip (Ship 3). I know that feels a little like "See Spot run," but novice Lenormand diviners must walk before they can run, right? What other sentence might you make from the cards appearing in this same order?

    OR:

    _____

    _____

    _____

2. Ship (3) / Rider (1) / Clover (2) = Someone from overseas (Ship 3) will arrive, bringing with him (Rider 1) an allergen (Clover 2) he managed to sneak through customs. Eww, right? But, still, that could be one meaning of this combination.

    OR:

    _____

    _____

    _____

3. Clover (2) / Ship (3) / Rider (1) = A happy surprise (Clover 2) of a surprise cruise (Ship 3) arrived (Rider 1).

    OR:

    _____

    _____

    _____

CHAPTER 2

House (4) / Tree (5) / Clouds (6)

House

4

CARD 4: HOUSE

(Abode, Home, Home Base, Safety, Familiarity, Comfort, Family)

There is something wholly satisfying about the fact that the House is the fourth card in the Lenormand deck: the number four denotes angles and corners, the things that constitute rooms with walls that hold and contain all things familiar, predictable, and domestic. In Lenormand, the House (4) is home, which, Robert Frost reminds us in his poem "The Death of the Hired Man," "is the place where, when you have to go there, / They have to take you in."

In reality, of course, home for many people can be an infinitely more complicated place than that. But in Lenormand, taken on its face, the House (4) represents as much that idealized version and vision of home as it does a physical structure. It represents the people with whom you live; it refers to a place of nurturance and sustenance. It is the place where trust and love abide. It is also the case, however, that the House (4) can morph into a place of danger and secrets, of arguments and simmering grudges. Alternatively, the House (4) can represent something in between those two widely and wildly opposite poles. As is always the case, the particular meaning of the House (4) will depend on the dance it does with the cards that surround it in a given spread. Generally speaking, though, when you think of the Lenormand House (4), your first association should be the archetype for the physical and emotional concept of home.

CARD 5: TREE

(Health, Genealogical Roots, Slow Growth, Patience, Steady Growth)

The Tree (5) in Lenormand is above all the card for health in all its forms—emotional, mental, spiritual, and physical. If one were doing a health reading, the surrounding cards would provide information as to which facet of health is being addressed, but the Tree (5) always seeks to remind us that health is something best considered from a holistic perspective of the body, mind, and spirit being inextricably intertwined. On the genealogical front, the Tree (5)'s significance is clear: roots beget a trunk, which begets branches, which beget leaves, which bear fruit. If the House (4) refers to the people with whom you live inside your actual house, the Tree (5) refers to the generations that both precede and follow you in your familial line. Quantum physics would assure us that healing, which is the primary meaning of the Tree (5), can be done backward and forward epigenetically, so that as we address our own ills and issues, our ancestors and our descendants can benefit from such healing work.

As wonderful a thought as that is, one must remember that the Tree (5) is a very slow-moving card. This should make infinite sense: Who among us would think to plant an acorn in our yard, go inside and brew a cup of tea, and then be shocked and angry when a full-grown oak tree had not sprung up in the time it took our water to boil? The Tree (5) reminds us that, once a seed is planted, much activity takes place under the soil. That activity's invisibility to the human eye does not make it any less complex and life-giving. The development of a root system is essential for any tree to flourish. The Tree (5) reminds us that healing is an inside job, that rot on the outside denotes greater rot on the inside, that things can sometimes look worse before they look better. The Tree (5) is the card of patience, care, attention, because those are the things that effect healing, growth, and strength.

Clouds

6

CARD 6: CLOUDS

(Doubts, Worry, Unclear Thinking, Depression, Dementia, Inclement Weather)

The Lenormand Clouds (6) is considered one of the negative cards in the deck by those who feel called upon to ascribe to each card such meanings as negative/positive/neutral. I don't know that I read them quite so rigidly, and I always bear in mind that any single card's meaning becomes clear only in the context of surrounding cards, but Clouds (6) is one of those cards whose meaning, on its face, is not wonderful. Clouds (6) is about thoughts, and the thoughts are either confused or else full of sadness or doubt. No less a wordsmith than William Shakespeare understood the meaning of Clouds (6): "There's nothing either good or bad, but thinking makes it so." (*Hamlet*, Act 2, Scene 2)

John Milton, in *Paradise Lost*, concurs: "The mind is its own place, and in itself can make a heaven of hell, a hell of heaven."

So the bad news about Clouds (6) is that this card connotes negative, doubtful, unclear thoughts. The good news about Clouds (6) is that when it appears, it is serving as a reminder to the sitter that Clouds (6) means *just* thoughts, the trajectory of which can be changed often simply with the setting of and commitment to that intention. The goal should be to sweep those Clouds (6) out to sea and to replace those thoughts with something more life- and hope-affirming.

In a health reading, however—especially for a person of some age and in combination with other particular cards—Clouds (6) can indicate dementia, which, as a rule, is intractable and progressive. And of course, where it indicates depression, professional intervention should be advised. Generally speaking, however, Clouds (6) is not a deal-breaker in a reading. This is simply a reminder that thoughts become things; that we cocreate our reality with the Universe; that if we seek a particular outcome, it is critical to help the Universe craft that for us by providing it with the right raw materials.

Some readers will tell you that if Clouds (6) has a dark side and a light side, you can determine which in a reading by whether these clouds are approaching or departing, but I like to get away from that soft literary racism which ascribes good to light and bad to dark. I also think that is a sort of . . . Taroistic way to read the card. In Lenormand, whether a Clouds (6) card has a light and dark side or it is a puff of wispy whiteness all throughout, a cloud is a cloud is a cloud: it is a frequently self-imposed impediment to clarity and wisdom and joy.

Its removal, through practice and habit and dint of will, can allow far lovelier, livelier things to move center stage. We can, as Milton says, make a heaven of hell by being aware of our thoughts and turning them in our preferred direction. That is a type of magic available to all of us who seek access to it.

The Clouds (6) card reminds us of our responsibility for our own state of mind. If we are able to banish the clouds ourselves, that is all to the good. If we need help with the banishing, we are asked to seek out that help. Some may have a biological makeup that involves omnipresent, low-lying cloud cover. If this is what the cards indicate, then ways to keep from being swallowed up by such cloud cover can be explored. The cards are always an ally. Even when cards deemed as negative pop up, the intention is never to cause dismay or feelings of futility in a sitter. Instead, such cards can remind us that the Universe sees and supports. Our ills are understood. I will teach you how to interpret such cards in a reading. My intention in this book is to show you how to partner with the cards so that they can show you the why and the how and the way through of any hardship, real or imagined. Now that we have explored another three cards, let's see how they might work in combination with each other, just as we did with the first three cards.

1. House (4) / Tree (5) / Clouds (6) = At home (House 4), there may be health issues (Tree 5), which cause worry (Clouds 6).

    OR:

    _____

    _____

    _____

2. Clouds (6) / House (4) / Tree (5) = It is doubtful (Clouds 6) that this house (House 4) will be one we stay in for a long time (Tree 5).

_____

_____

_____

Now you try your hand at two different interpretations for the cards
in this order:

3.   Tree (5) / Clouds (6) / House (4) =

_____

_____

_____

OR:

_____

_____

_____

CHAPTER 3

Snake (7) / Coffin (8) / Bouquet (9)

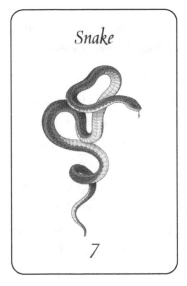

CARD 7: SNAKE

(Problem, Complication, Clever Woman, Same-Sex Relationship, Intestines, Digestive Tract)

The Lenormand Snake (7) is a card truly reflective of the time during which this divination system was devised. For all who might be tempted to see it as Kundalini energy or as transformation, let me say, without equivocation, that this is not that. As you become more fluent and adept at reading Lenormand, your understanding of card meanings will expand and grow. Your personal connection with the cards will dictate the extent to which this happens. Nevertheless, each card functions within a system governed by parameters and perimeters that must be observed if one is to be true to the Lenormand way of reading. These are not Tarot or oracle cards. The rules of reading Lenormand are particular to Lenormand. So, if the Snake (7) is neither Kundalini energy nor transformation, what is it?

The Snake (7)'s most common meaning is indeed the first key-word listed above: a Snake (7) indicates some sort of problem. This understanding of the Snake (7) is practically instinctual in human beings, ophidiophiles (snake lovers) notwithstanding. The Bible itself seeks to explain this general and natural antipathy. Of course, its explanation is in the context of explaining God's punishment exacted upon the Garden of Eden's snake, which tempted Eve who tempted Adam and set the whole ball rolling downhill, I guess one could say. This quote from Genesis tells the tale. The "I" here is God's own Self. The one to whom God speaks is the Snake:

And I will put enmity between thee and the woman, and between your seed and her seed; it shall bruise thy head and thou shalt bruise his heel. (Genesis 3:15)

This *enmity* is meant to be for all time, so please, when you encounter the Snake (7) in a reading, let your first inclination be to look to the other cards in the spread to help you determine the nature and extent of the problem that the Snake (7) card, more often than not, portends. But not always . . .

As even more evidence that Lenormand is a product of its time, it is occasionally the case that the Snake (7) is not a problem, but is instead a clever woman. The irony that a clever woman would, in some quarters, be considered synonymous with a problem should, of course, be lost on no one. What can I tell you? It is not the case that the Snake (7) has never appeared this way for me in a reading. It has, but very seldom. The lesson here is to never assume. Always let the other cards in the spread direct your understanding as to which meaning any given card is taking—including that old Snake (7).

I have listed a third meaning for Snake (7) that warrants some discussion here. Again, as a product of its time, a traditional Lenormand deck has a grand total of four people, and that is if you count the person riding the horse in the Rider (1) card as one of the four, even though he/she is incidental to the message they carry. Each Lenormand deck has a Man (28) and a Woman (29) and a Child (13) card also. I bring up the Man (28) and the Woman (29) because they are relevant to the third meaning of the Snake (7), which is a same-sex relationship. I realized the relevance of this meaning during a startling encounter early in my public reading career.

A client at the little shop where I read sat down and asked me about a relationship she was in. Generally, all I ask of a sitter is the area of their lives which they would like me to use my cards to explore with them. With no more information than that, I began to pull the cards. While it was obvious that there were significant issues in this relationship, there were other cards in the spread that clearly showed me the nature of these problems. The Snake (7) was there, but I had the distinct feeling that it was playing a different role in the spread than illustrating a problem. I looked from my cards to my sitter and back again, biting my lip, and wondering whether to say what I was being given by that Snake (7). Finally, I asked my client if they were in a same-sex relationship, and they confirmed that was the case. It was the Snake (7) that told me so. It was a wonderful reminder to just listen to what I am given, to not censor the message, except insofar as I try to craft it into words that are hearable and receivable by my sitter, and to trust Spirit as my partner in every reading. This was years ago. Fortunately, modern decks now include, as a matter of course, two men cards and two women cards. This means that, more often than not, a same-sex relationship will be evident through the presence of these cards, and the Snake (7) card becomes free to abdicate that role and stick to the two first meanings I provided: problem or clever woman. Do remember, moving forward, that nine times out of ten, Snake (7) is indeed a problem. But be open to the once in a while when it appears in its other form. Reading with a light touch will always inform you which is which and when. If your reading has to do with health, let me remind you that in the definitions for this card, Snake (7) can refer to issues with the intestines. Let me also remind you that you will not be able to tell this unless you read the Snake (7) alongside other cards in the spread that would lead you in that direction. It is neither desirable nor necessary to leap to conclusions on the basis of any single card. It is the grouping of cards together that tell any story.

Coffin

8

CARD 8: COFFIN

(Endings, Death, Depression, Exhaustion, Illness, Boredom, Claustrophobia, Transformation)

Whenever the Coffin (8) shows up in a reading, I watch my sitter's eyes widen in trepidation. Always, that prompts me to quip, "Nobody likes a coffin, right?" You may well be thinking the same thing, but here's something to consider: just as I told you that nine times out of ten, the Snake (7) portends a problem, it has also been my experience that 99.9% of the time, the Coffin (8) does *not* portend death. In fact, the only time I would be tempted to interpret this card as death is when it is paired in a reading with the Lily (30). More about that later, of course. The point here is that when your sitter sees the Coffin (8), they will immediately leap to a doomsday scenario. As a reader, you will be tempted to go to the same place. I encourage you to temper that instinct and see what the Coffin (8)'s sister cards have to say in the spread, so that you do not misspeak.

Now that that huge caveat is out of the way, we can explore the Coffin (8) more closely. The first, most common meaning of the card is endings. Exactly what is ending will be indicated by the other cards in a given spread. Endings may perhaps sound negative to you, but is it not true that an infinite number of things have both beginnings and endings? If it is a good thing that is ending, that can make us sad and wistful, of course. But what about the fact that bad things can end too? In such cases, the Coffin (8) can be a welcome card indeed.

There's a spiritual I love a lot, because this is its refrain:

I'm so glad trouble don't last always.

I love it because it is a reminder that even during times of treading the most roiling waters, times when we see no lighthouse or buoy on our horizon, we can rest in the awareness that "the only constant is change." Therefore, if there is no other single thing about which we can rejoice, we can rejoice in the fact that "trouble don't last always." Very often this is the message of the Coffin (8).

Returning to the Coffin (8)'s more disquieting meanings, it is definitely the card for illness or exhaustion. Because a coffin is actually a box, it is also the card for feeling boxed in, confined, or depressed. As ever, the other cards in a spread will help you discern which of these roles the Coffin (8) plays, but there is one more meaning of the Coffin (8) that is absolutely worthy of further exploration.

If you recall, in my discussion of Snake (7), I implored you not to think of it as the card for transformation. This is because that role is reserved for the Coffin (8). You may well wonder how it is that a card whose meanings include illness, confinement, depression, and yes, sometimes death itself, can also signify transformation. It is actually quite logical.

Physics tells us that matter can be neither created nor destroyed. What matter is capable of doing, however, is *changing its form*. Take water, for example: Water can change from liquid to solid (ice) to gas (steam). It can even change color and create of itself intricate geometric shapes in the form of snowflakes. In every case, water is called by a different name, because of its different form, but its essence stays the same, whether it is dew or hail or ice or snow or vapor. For the creators of Lenormand, and certainly for this diviner, these principles extend to . . . everything. Even in that spiritual, where the singer rejoices in the fact that "trouble don't last always," the troubled state can shift, morph, transform into its opposite, which is joy.

When the Coffin (8) shows up in your reading, please put transformation high on your list of possible interpretations; certainly place it higher on your list than death. The Coffin (8) indicates that something must end, certainly. But that is only so that transformation can occur. One thing cannot be two things simultaneously. Or can it? Ice is just water, frozen. Steam is just water, vaporized. The soul is the soul, always, but it can transform from embodied to disembodied; it exists, nevertheless. Allow the Coffin (8) to fill you with curiosity, rather than dread. And if it does appear as illness, confinement, depression, the Coffin (8)'s sister cards can advise as to how such travails may be navigated, so that you and your sitter are reassured.

CARD 9: BOUQUET

(Gift, Reward, Promotion, Visual and Performing Arts, Beauty, Girl)

It is with no small sense of relief that we now turn from discussions of snakes and coffins to contemplation of the perennially positive Bouquet (9). The is the second of the three "happiness cards," which is my term for the Clover (2), a card with which we have already spent time; the Bouquet (9), our current card; and Lily (30), to which I have earlier referred and at which we will look in depth later on. Each of these three cards denotes a different type of happiness for me. Clover (2), as discussed, is quick, giddy, and often serendipitous. The Bouquet (9) is a variation on the happiness theme and refers to rewards and gifts. When Bouquet (9) appears in a reading with Clover (2), the reward or gift will be doubly delightful for its unexpectedness.

There is more to the Bouquet (9), however. It is the card for all visual and performing arts: music, sculpture, painting, drama, photography—all are represented by the Bouquet (9). However, this card is just as likely to represent hairdressing or dog grooming or interior design. It is the card for anything that lends beauty and ease to the world in the forms of those things our senses receive. The Bouquet (9), in combination with, for example, the Bear (15), can even represent food, so long as it is artfully and lovingly prepared and plated and presented. So even our mouths may receive the beauty and ease of the Bouquet (9). Also, isn't this obviously one of the words we use for a pleasant aroma? And, of course, sometimes a Bouquet (9) is a literal bouquet: an arrangement of flowers that delights both our eyes and noses. As always, I encourage you to relax and not recoil at the fact that the Bouquet (9) can be so many things. I remind you here—as I have before, and as I will again and again—that the exact role for the Bouquet (9) in a given spread is determined largely by the cards with which it appears. The other cards are always excellent droppers of bread crumbs so that your reading direction will be clear and unimpeded, so long as you know the cards and so long as you see with a third eye and listen with a third ear to the information you are given.

Because the Bouquet (9) is such a lovely card, I arrived at another meaning for it early in my reading career. Before people began to chase me down for readings, I would chase them down and beg them to let me read for them. No one could escape me. I was all about practice, practice, practice, which is, of course, how anyone gets good at anything. One of my earliest and most frequent sitters was my then-teenaged daughter. In fact, Lenormand became the village that helped me finish raising her once her father had passed away. Because my daughter was fifteen, I did not feel comfortable using Child (13) when doing a reading for or about her. And I certainly did not feel inclined to use Woman (29), as really, she was betwixt and between the two. The Bouquet (9) became the card I used to read for her and for all subsequent teenage girls who seek me out. It is a card that speaks to the first, earliest blush of womanhood, with all its promise and potential. My daughter and other young sitters love the idea of this card representing them. I hope they take it as it is meant: a small and simple gesture to show them that I see them; something to put them and me at ease, so that any messages I have for them are effortlessly delivered and willingly received.

There are no negative associations with the Bouquet (9) itself. It is the case, however, that things such as false flattery, transactional relationships, manipulative giving and gifting can all be a part of a spread's meaning when the Bouquet (9) appears along with more difficult, ill-freighted cards. For now, though, we will let the Bouquet (9) stand alone and be the beautiful gift, the well-earned reward, the representation of all we are and all we do to make the world a place of light and goodness.

· · ·

Now, for a look at these last three cards in combination:

1. Snake (7) / Coffin (8) / Bouquet (9) = A problem (Snake 7) ends (Coffin 8) in a way that feels like a gift (Bouquet 9).

    OR:

    _____

    _____

    _____

2. Bouquet (9) / Snake (7) / Coffin (8) = A promotion (Bouquet 9) is more trouble (Snake 7) than gift and will lead to the recipient feeling boxed in and bored (Coffin 8).

    OR:

_____

_____

_____

Now, try your hand at this combination, coming up with two possible interpretations.

3. Coffin (8) / Bouquet (9) / Snake (7) =

_____

_____

    OR:

_____

_____

_____

CHAPTER 4

Any Card as Significator

Now that we have walked our way though the first nine cards—taking us a quarter of the way through the deck—it is time to stretch our knowledge by allowing the cards to dance with new partners. Already you have learned to read the basic three-card spread. Essentially, you have looked at each three-card grouping as a sentence, with the first card serving as the subject and the other two cards modifying, describing, or explaining in some way the circumstances surrounding that first subject card. Effectively, it is as though the second card of a given trio acts as the verb, with the third card as adjective or adverb. This is indeed how most three-card spreads work. You can see that a three-card spread can provide certain information, but the very human tendency of any novice reader will be to try and pile more into those three cards than is actually there. This would be a mistake. It is the beginner reader's error of calling upon one's ego to provide information one may feel is lacking. This is not how Lenormand is read. The ego must be put aside, and the cards allowed to tell the story. There are several ways to make easier this jettisoning of ego in favor of magic making. Here are a few:

A cardinal rule of Lenormand is that cards are not meant to be thrown, drawn, pulled in a vacuum. In order for Lenormand to do its best work, the cards are meant to be laid out in the context of an asked question. A sitter's question is a reader's most helpful tool, as it is the question that gives the spread you lay both context and direction. As a reader, I am a big proponent of using a significator. The term refers to a card you will select at the beginning of a session to represent the area into which your sitter would like you to delve. For example, if you are reading on health, your significator would be the Tree (5). If you are reading on a move/relocation, then the Ship (3) would be your significator. There is absolutely no question a sitter can ask for which you will not be able to choose a significator. That is why memorization of the multiple and often disparate meanings of each card is essential in order to do the work well. Let's look at this more closely.

Say that your sitter is inquiring as to whether or not they will receive a promotion at work. The first thing I would do is consider which card might best represent a promotion, and the Bouquet (9) is the card that I would choose. Now that I have selected my significator, the Bouquet (9) can only serve as the card for the promotion. It cannot simultaneously assume any of its other keyword meanings, which is quite a helpful thing. The Bouquet (9) now has parameters drawn around it. I am certain of one important thing in the reading so far, and that is that I know the meaning of the Bouquet (9) in any spread I draw on this question for this sitter. It will stand for the promotion, and nothing else. Now that you have a question and a card to represent the subject of the question, any other cards you will draw will be interpreted in the context of the question. Knowing question and context can set you quite far down the road toward an accurate and satisfying reading for your sitter. Here is an example:

Say you are asked this promotion question, and you pull Bouquet (9) / Snake (7) / Clouds (6). It would be clear to you at once that this promotion (Bouquet 9) would be doubtful (Clouds 6) because someone or something would have interfered, causing a problem (Snake 7). As we currently have learned the first nine cards of the deck, now would be a good time to introduce cards which we have not yet seen dance together. Sticking with these nine, let's mix them up a bit, staying with our sitter's question about a job promotion. As you will recall, our nine cards so far are: Rider (1), Clover (2), Ship (3), House (4), Tree (5), Clouds (6), Snake (7), Coffin (8), Bouquet (9).

If we were to pull Rider (1) / Clover (2) / Bouquet (9), we would say: News (Rider 1) of a fortuitous (Clover 2) type will arrive soon (Clover 2 is a quick-moving card) about a promotion (Bouquet 9). Such a reading would be good news for our sitter!

OR

House (4) / Snake (7) / Clouds (6): Someone else in-house at the company (House 4) may also be under consideration, causing a problem (Snake 7) for the sitter by putting any promotion in doubt (Clouds 6).

OR

Rider (1) / Ship (3) / Tree (5): Your sitter will receive word (Rider 1) that progress (Ship 3) on this promotion will take a while (Tree 5). Notice that in these last two examples, the Bouquet (9) does not appear at all. Nevertheless, we are only interested in the job promotion as our subject, so it remains the implicit subject of the reading, regardless of the cards we draw.

OR

Bouquet (9) / Clover (2) / Coffin (8): The promotion (Bouquet 9) is on a track to move quickly in the sitter's favor (Clover 2) and will have a transformative effect (Coffin 8) on the sitter's career.

Here is a caveat: you may have been tempted, with this last example, to think that Coffin (8) implies that any promotion comes to a screeching halt. After all, is a Coffin (8) not an ending? This is where you, as a reader, must use discernment, a very light touch, and an ear open to the guidance of the Universe. Our sitter here, of course, is imaginary, but when you have a real person across from you, there will be something energetic operating, if you allow this to be the case, such that you will be able to easily ascertain whether that Coffin

(8) portends doom or career ascendance. Practice and trusting what information you receive will show you the difference.

Let us pose another question. Your sitter asks, "Why is my friend so depressed?"

The Coffin (8) is the card for depression, so if we wanted to choose it as our significator, we certainly could pull that card first intentionally and then see what cards follow. But I'd like to change things up and not pull a significator. This means that we will simply pull cards at random. I hasten to add here that random does not actually mean random. We will be pulling cards with the sitter's question in mind, and with the intention that, whatever cards appear, they address that question in a way that is helpful and clear. What if we were to pull Rider (1) / Ship (3) / Clouds (6)? We might read this as: The friend received news (Rider 1) that a trip (Ship 3) she had planned was now in doubt (Clouds 8). Certainly, that would be cause for a bad mood!

OR

Tree (5) / Snake (7) / House (4): Health problems, such as COVID concerns (Tree 5/Snake 7) have kept her stuck at home (House 4).

You see how helpful it is to have a question? We know from our sitter that the friend is depressed. Therefore, there will be no option to interpret any of the cards in a positive light. Even cards with inherently positive meanings must bow to the authority of the question. So, if Bouquet (9) or Clover (2), for example, were to turn up in answer to this question, we would have to view these cards in the question's context and assume these cards' natural positivity was thwarted in some way, thus explaining the depression. Therefore, Clover (2) / Bouquet (9) / Rider (1) would need to be read as more aspirational than actual. Therefore, as an answer to the question "Why is my friend depressed?" these three cards would indicate that the friend *expected* some happy news or outcome. The fact that we know from the question that she is depressed intimates that the expected good news did not, in fact, materialize; hence the depression. See how three "happy cards" were able to answer a question for which we might have expected to see more negative cards? The cards will always answer your question, if you understand that sometimes it is necessary to dig a little deeper than the surface in order to discover the nuanced answer.

CHAPTER 5

Scythe (10) / Whip (11) / Birds (12)

Scythe

10

CARD 10: SCYTHE

(Decision, Sudden or Abrupt Ending, Surgery, Injection, Murder, Cutting, Reaping)

The first thing to learn about the Scythe (10) is how the word is meant to be pronounced: the *c* is silent. All you are meant to hear at the beginning of the word is the *s*. After the *s*, think of the thing you see out of: your eye. After that, pretend you have a lisp as you pronounce the *th*. The final *e*, just like the *c*, is silent. So the word is pronounced *s-eye-th*. You're welcome!

With pronunciation out of the way, you may be wondering what exactly a scythe is. Technically speaking, it is a dual-purpose farm implement, consisting of a long handle topped by a curved blade. The handle is what one uses to wield the scythe, of course, and the blade itself is meant to cut grain. The blade is curved to facilitate gathering up the cut grain so that it can be efficiently transferred to where it will be baled and carted for further processing elsewhere.

The language of Lenormand takes full advantage of this tool's dual identity as both cutter and gatherer in ways that are quite brilliant. Firstly, and most frequently, when it appears in a Lenormand reading, the Scythe (10) refers to a decision. There is a forthright resolution implicit in Scythe (10), a recognition that someone has come down on a particular side of an issue, about which there will be no further equivocation or fence-sitting. When I see this card, I immediately think of the mid-20th-century actor Yul Brynner, who played the Pharaoh Rameses in the blockbuster film *The Ten Commandments* and declared, "So it is written. So it shall be done." Just as no one would think to argue with a pharaoh, the Scythe (10) is unequivocal in its certitude. While there may be different opinions bandied back and forth, once the Scythe (10) appears, the message is clear: the Scythe (10) brooks no debate.

While decisiveness certainly has the capacity to be a positive attribute in a person, it is also the case that there is (pardon the pun) *an edge* to the Scythe (10). It can be (again, I ask your pardon) *cutting*. This sharpness can refer to tone, language, and message, of course, when the Scythe (10) is about conversation. The Scythe (10), though, also refers to the literal sharpness of an injection, surgery, stabbing, slicing. Whether the Scythe (10) is describing a decision, cutting commentary, a surgeon's careful and precise skill, or a killer's wild wielding will depend, as always, on the surrounding cards. But recall that the Scythe (10) is more than a cutting thing. The blade of the Scythe (10) is curved, and so sometimes this card is about gathering, amassing, reaping, bringing in. Cutting and gathering are opposites, of course, and so how one determines whether the card represents the one or the other is by assessing its relationship to the other cards in a given spread.

There is a school of thought among some Lenormand readers that you can determine which meaning to ascribe to the Scythe (10) according to which way the blade is curving. This is the same school which says that one can determine whether something positive or negative is on the horizon by which side of the Clouds (6) card is light and which side is dark. I do not subscribe to that school of thought. I think it is a "Taroistic" way to read the cards because it makes the artist's rendition central to the understanding of the card. Lenormand, although it is indeed a divination system comprised of pictures, is not meant to be read imagistically, as Tarot is, but is rather a linguistic language, where the words are all-important. All a reader needs to know are the words Scythe (10) or Clouds (6) in order to summon up connotations that are relevant to the question and the reading. This is why, if you simply memorized the thirty-six Lenormand card numbers, you would be able to do an accurate and even profound reading, regardless of which way a Scythe (10) blade or a Clouds (6)'s light side is facing. Directionality is important, but only in regard to where a card appears relative to other cards. Directionality within a particular card is less important, in my way of reading. Just as a Clouds (6) is a Clouds (6), a Scythe (10) is a Scythe (10). It is enough to assess whether we are indeed talking about a decision, a cutting comment, a surgeon's scalpel, or a murderer's switchblade. And remember, the sister cards that appear with that Scythe (10) in a reading will always guide us in the right direction.

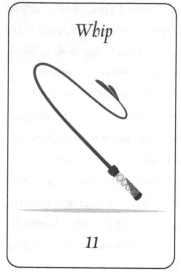

Whip

11

CARD 11: WHIP

(Sex, Arguments, Repetition, Discipline, Athlete, Writer)

The Whip (11) is a card on which you will see portrayed either an actual, easily identifiable whip or a pair of brooms, in which case the card may be "Birches." Either way, the meanings for the card will be the same. And either way, the card is fascinating because of its disparate meanings.

Whether we are talking about Birches (11) or Whips (11), there is no denying that there is a certain intensity, and even a potential harshness, to this card. This card, which I will call the Whip (11), is one of the two cards in the deck that represent sex. As you might expect, this is the kind of sex that is hungry, impatient, urgent. At least, that is how I read it. I don't think that needs further elaboration. Right?

The Whip (11) is also the card for heated conversations—arguments, even. When paired with the Scythe (10), the language of such arguments can well include the unkind, cutting language into which arguments sometimes devolve. Without the presence of Scythe (10) or Snake (7), however, an argument, as portrayed by Whip (11), can simply reference a strong difference of opinion, an intense dialogical back-and-forth.

Because a whip is an instrument—a weapon, really—wielded over and over again, this is also the card for repetition. For example, in a reading on health, you might see Tree (5) / Clover (2) / Whip (11) and accurately suspect that the issue at hand is seasonal allergies.

Tree (5) = Health / Clover (2) = Allergy / Whip (11) = Seasonal, Recurring

The Whip (11) is also, for obvious reasons, the card for discipline, of both others and the self. Therefore, it is the card representing the athlete as well as the writer. The Whip (11) reminds us that simply wishing for something is not enough. A wish must be yoked to intention and action in order for that wish to come to fruition. An athlete must put time in on the track or field or in the gym consistently, day after day, in order to achieve peak performance. A writer must show up at the yellow legal pad or the keyboard according to a regular schedule, whether or not they feel the spark of inspiration. It is in going through the motions of showing up and sitting in the chair day after day after day (Whip 11) that novels are written, poetry is crafted, and characters in a play are brought to life. Such discipline does not always feel good, but its consequences are always satisfying and character building. Medicine need not taste good to work. But neither must self-discipline feel bad. Stretching and strengthening the muscles or the mind are always worth the effort. In a spread on the subject, the location of the Whip (11) and the cards that surround it can indicate whether the effort being exerted is insufficient, too much, or just enough. Whip (11) / Bouquet (9), for example, would remind a sitter that their hard work and dedication are being rewarded. Pleasure and pain are not unrelated, as we know. In regard to self-discipline, the Whip (11) can be instructive as to proper dosage for optimum outcome.

Birds

12

CARD 12: BIRDS

(Communication, Conversation, Meetings, Gossip, Buzz, Advertising, Sorrow)

Although it is most often the case that the Birds (12) card will portray sparrows or robins, once in a while owls will be an artist's bird of choice. If you have a deck where owls are on card 12, be careful not to succumb to the temptation to imbue the card with a meaning that Lenormand does not ascribe to it. We tend to associate owls with wisdom, but that has no relevance at all to the Lenormand Birds (12). Just let those owls be Birds (12) for the purposes of your readings.

Nearly always, there will be more than one bird on the card, regardless of bird type. That is because Birds (12) is the card for communication, conversations, and meetings, none of which can take place in a vacuum. Such activities require that two or more be gathered together. These gatherings can take place in person or over the phone, but they involve the use of the voice, as the communication is always verbal and oral. There is no particular value assessment, either good or bad, attached to this card. The conversations to which Birds (12) refers to can be casual or consequential; catty or concerned. A board meeting or a backyard gossip session between neighbors and across a fence could both be referenced by Birds (12). In a reading in which a sitter asks how they might improve their business, Birds (12) appearing may suggest that the sitter ought to give deeper consideration to an advertising and marketing strategy. All verbal communication comes under the heading of Birds (12), no matter its nature or content.

Here is an odd thing, though: although this interpretation comes up very rarely for me, another significant meaning of Birds (12) is, of all things, sorrow. In fact, I know many European Lenormand readers for whom sorrow is the first and foremost meaning of Birds (12). Certainly, you can set that intention for the card in your deck, if the idea appeals to you. I did not, as there are other cards in the deck that serve that purpose of naming sorrow for me, so when Birds (12) does pop up as sorrow in one of my readings, I am always surprised. You may well wonder what I mean by "pop up."

If I am doing a reading and it is clear from the surrounding cards that Birds (12) cannot possibly be referring to conversations or meetings, I will look to see if sorrow fits the scenario in the spread in front of me. The lesson here is that good and accurate reading requires flexibility. Many of the Lenormand cards have multiple meanings that are unrelated one to another. While this can be a source of great frustration for the novice reader, it is invariably the case that with time, practice, a light hand, and an open third eye and third ear, meaning will begin to coalesce like . . . magic.

• • •

Now, for some practice:

1. Scythe (10) / Whip (11) / Birds (12) = Cutting words (Scythe 10) during a heated argument (Whip 11) caused her great sorrow (Birds 12).

    OR:

    _____

    _____

    _____

2. Birds (12) / Scythe (10) / Whip (11) = After the meeting (Birds 12), he decided (Scythe 10) to take a more disciplined approach (Whip 10) to the project.

   OR:

   _____

   _____

   _____

Try this last trio on your own, coming up with two alternate meanings for this combination:

3. Whip (11) / Birds (12) / Scythe (10) =

   _____

   _____

   _____

   OR:

   _____

   _____

   _____

CHAPTER 6

Five- and Seven-Card Spreads, Significator Practice, Mirroring

Now that we are fully one-third through the deck, it is time to expand our three-card spreads to five and then seven cards. This will also be an opportunity to practice using a significator, a technique I taught you earlier. We will additionally examine a technique called mirroring. Both will be useful tools to add to your Lenormand skill set.

Let us begin with a refresher on significator cards. Any card in a Lenormand deck has the ability to serve as a significator, which is a card chosen to represent the subject of your reading. Often, readers will decide to select Card 28 (Man) or Card 29 (Woman) as the significator representing their sitter. That is a perfectly fine way to approach a reading, but if someone is sitting at your table for a reading, is it not a given that the reading will be for them? That said, it can indeed be both challenging and exciting to use the Man (28) or Woman (29) card as your significator, because as you pull the rest of the cards for the spread, you have no idea what subject area of the sitter's life the cards will bring up. Generally speaking, what will reveal itself is what the sitter most needs to hear. For the novice reader, however, it is always helpful to receive a little more specific guidance when beginning a reading. Your sitter may well have a pressing issue that has brought them to your table. Since a reading lasts for a pre-determined length of time, it can be beneficial to both you and your sitter if you ask them what area of their life they would like to explore. Based on your sitter's answer, you can then select a more specific and appropriate significator for the spread.

For example, let's say your sitter has put a bid on a new house and is curious as to whether the bid will be accepted. In that case, Card 4 (House) could be your significator. If your sitter wanted to ask a question related to health, then Card 5 (Tree) would be the significator you would choose. If their health question were more specific, as in wondering how an upcoming surgery would go, then you might select Card 10 (Scythe) as your significator. If they wanted to know if they would receive a job promotion, then Card 9 (Bouquet) is the one you would choose.

Let's try a sample question to see how the significator functions. We will look at that first question about whether or not our sitter's bid on a house will be accepted. If one were to answer the question without a significator, one would simply shuffle the deck and draw five cards. Using a significator, however, one would shuffle the deck as usual, and then turn over the cards individually until reaching the House (4). That card would go in the center of the table. Then, the two cards that preceded the House (4) in the deck would be placed to the left, and the two cards following the House (4) would be placed to the right, thus completing our traditional Lenormand Line of Five. Let's say the spread came out this way:

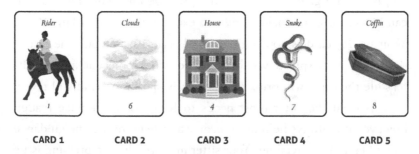

CARD 1   CARD 2   CARD 3   CARD 4   CARD 5

The Language of Lenormand

Rider (1) / Clouds (6) / House (4) / Snake (7) / Coffin (8)

At first glance, would you say that the offer that your sitter made on the new house will be accepted or not? If you were to construct a sentence from the cards, you might come up with this:

News (Rider 1) of a doubtful nature (Clouds 6) will come in about the bid (House 4), indicating that there's been a problem (Snake 7) and the bid will not be accepted (Coffin 8).

BUT

What if you pulled these cards instead:

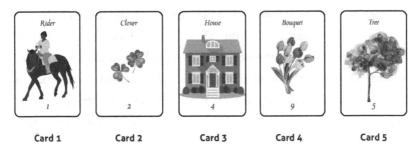

| Card 1 | Card 2 | Card 3 | Card 4 | Card 5 |

Rider (1) / Clover (2) / House (4) / Bouquet (9) / Tree (5)

Fortunate, happy news (Rider 1/Clover 2) about the house bid (House 4) will arrive, indicating that the bid has been accepted, and your hard work will be rewarded (Bouquet 9) because you will be putting down roots (Tree 5) in this new home.

In each reading, since the House (4) is the significator, every other card will be read in the context of the question about the house bid. One reading was decidedly pessimistic, while the other was unmistakably optimistic. The answer as to whether or not the bid would be accepted was up in the air until the other cards were drawn, but it is the significator House (4) that contextualizes, grounds, and clarifies what the subject of the reading will be. I would encourage you to explore the many ways in which each card in the Lenormand deck can serve as a spread significator and to use the keywords provided for each card to help inform you as to what sorts of significators there might be.

MIRRORING

Lines of Five and of Seven can employ the mirroring technique.

The first five-card spread above was Rider (1) / Clouds (6) / House (4) / Snake (7) / Coffin (8). With the mirroring technique, we don't just look at the cards in linear order, but we do a further assessment by pondering pairs of cards. Here, the cards we are able to mirror in this spread are Rider (1) / Coffin (8) and then Clouds (6) / Snake (7). These pairs tell us that the news (Rider 1) will be depressing (Coffin 8) and that the deal is in doubt (Clouds 6) because of some problem that arose with the bid (Snake 7). Thus, we have confirmed our first negative impression of the spread because of the further detail that mirroring provides.

Conversely, with the second spread of Rider (1) / Clover (2) / House (4) / Bouquet (9) / Tree (5), we are able to mirror Rider (1) / Tree (5) to learn that news (Rider 1) will come telling the sitter they can put down roots (Tree 5) in this new place. Further, with the mirroring of Clover (2) together with Bouquet (9) we can assure our sitter that this good news will arrive with alacrity (Clover 2) and will feel like a well-earned reward (Bouquet 9).

No sitter would be satisfied with a simple yes or no answer to their query. Using a Line of Five spread and incorporating mirroring into the reading will provide your sitter with both the yes/no they are looking for as well as some fleshed-out detail that they will appreciate.

The Line of Seven simply requires the adding on of two more cards to your five-card spread. I think it is a good rule of thumb to decide in advance whether you will be throwing five or seven cards. In the case of the seven-card spread, and using the above examples, one would know in advance that the reading has to do with a housing situation. Just as before, one would shuffle the cards, and then one at a time turn them over, until the House (4) appears. Placing that in the center of your table, just as before, one would then place to the left of the House (4) the three cards that preceded it in the deck. To round out the line of seven, one would take the three cards following the House (4) in the deck, and place them in order to the right of the House (4). You now have more information, and you also have more cards to mirror to receive yet more guidance. In the positions 1, 2, 3, 4, 5, 6, 7, you are able to mirror cards 1 and 7, cards 2 and 6, and cards 3 and 5. The only card that cannot be mirrored is the center card, but as that card stands for the subject of your reading, there is no need to mirror it. What you want to do with mirroring is to look at the pairs of cards mentioned to get extra or confirmatory information about that center card.

CHAPTER 7

Child (13) / Fox (14) / Bear (15)

Child

13

CARD 13: CHILD

(Baby, Beginner, Tyro, Child, Start, New, Small, Immaturity)

The Child (13) features a male or female child, depending on the artist's preference. Some more modern decks will have two cards to choose from, and the age of the child on the card can vary from infancy to nearly adolescent. Even though this is one of the few "people" cards in a Lenormand deck, the card seldom refers to a specific person. Most often, it instead represents something small or in the beginning stages, and it can be a reminder to the sitter not to bite off more than they can chew. When paired or mirroring another card that suggests something wonderful, such as Clover (2) or Bouquet (9) for example, the Child (13) actually serves to scale down expectations of the occasion's or circumstance's magnitude. For example, you may win the lottery—a fortuitous event indeed—and perhaps foretold by Clover (6). But if Child (13) also appears in the line announcing this happy windfall, you may not count on being able to quit your day job based on the win. A lottery win Clover (2) is wonderful, but Child (13) reminds you to manage your expectations in regard to what that win will allow you to do.

Child (13) can also be a descriptor for an adult who is, in the best circumstance, childlike, trusting, and naive. In the worst scenario, this card can describe an adult who is childish, immature, and petulant. For example, in a seven-card spread in which you have chosen to use Man (28) as your significator, if the surrounding cards were lined up as Snake (7) / Fox (14) / Child (13) / Man (28) / Mountain (21) / Scythe (10) / Whip (11), you might well suspect this man to be, at the very least, unpleasant to be around, insistent on getting his own way, and certainly immature. Children, as wonderful as they can be, are not always so. Similarly, the Child (13) is multidimensional and must be interpreted in the context of any accompanying cards if the nature of this card is to be accurately understood.

Fox

14

CARD 14: FOX

(Job, Foreigner, Doctor/Specialist, Professor, Detective, Circumspection, Suspicion, Distrust, Self-Interest, Subterfuge)

A fox is an animal that is not easily taken unawares. Always looking out for self, the fox is a wary animal. It can see around every corner and will leverage every advantage. Even though I mention wariness in relation to Fox (14), it is important to understand the value of circumspection, careful planning, and self-interest. The naivete implicit in Child (13) can be charming, but exercised at the wrong time and in the wrong place it can have dire consequences.

We all need to have a little Fox (14) inside us that we can pull out when we need to be guarded, suspicious, or simply aware of our surroundings. Not everything that everyone says can be taken at face value. Fox (14) reminds us of this tendency in other people, and of the fact that it is also a human tendency we also share. This card's bent is toward self-interest. Self-interest is not necessarily nefarious, but it can be.

Do you recall my story about my young sitter who asked how her blind date would go? Now that we have more cards to work with, let's look at the question again. Let's say we pull this five-card spread:

Clover (2) / Bouquet (9) / Fox (14) / Clouds (6) / Snake (7).

Let's say our young sitter asks if this blind date will prove to be their Prince Charming. What would you say? Clover (2) speaks to the element of surprise always inherent in any blind date. We do not want to be too quick to make an assessment just because Clover (2) is generally a happy, fun card denoting luck. But the Clover (2) is followed by the Bouquet (9), so our diviner's senses perk up and start to move in the direction of thinking that perhaps this blind date could indeed lead to a fairy-tale ending. The Bouquet (9) implies that this mystery person will not be at all hard on the eyes, so that is a relief. Perhaps they will even literally come bearing the gift of flowers. Everything is lovely so far. But this is not the end of the reading, as we have three more cards to factor in. The next card is the Fox (14). As a reader, your warning bells should immediately go off at this point. Of all the cards that might have shown up right in the center of the spread, that Fox (14) implies that all is not as it appears. Did not Red Riding Hood's "grandmother" turn out to be a wolf in disguise? Is not a wolf at least cousin to the fox? But we don't want to jump to conclusions. After all, the Fox (14) is also the card for a doctor who is a specialist and for the scientist or detective who needs a careful and discerning eye. Also the Fox (14) is the card for someone from a different country. Perhaps this blind date is simply a medical specialist or a secret agent with a charming foreign accent, right? But we have yet more cards to read in this spread before we leap to that conclusion. The fourth card in our spread is Clouds (6). This card casts a pall over the first two cheery cards, and it could well be that the cards are warning our sitter to listen to their own sixth-sense doubts about this stranger. Remember, the Fox (14) can be both the person with ill intent and the person who suspects such ill intent. Clouds (6) ought to make our sitter's eyes narrow as a fox's might, instead of widen at that big Bouquet (9) borne by the Fox (14). What kind of transactional gift might that Bouquet (9) actually be? The spread's final card tells the tale: the Snake (7) is up to no good at all. This blind date will not prove to be Prince Charming, even if they are a world-renowned specialist with a dreamy accent.

Our sitter is warned by this spread to make sure there is no second date with this Fox (14), as the latter's intent may well not be honorable. Our sitter is reminded that they, too, can be the Fox (14) and use their intuition to ferret out danger before it occurs. Maybe being a no-show would be our sitter's best course of action. That way, our foxy sitter would outfox that Fox (14). Isn't Lenormand terrific?

On a way more banal note, the Fox (14) is also the card for one's day-to-day job, the work one does to earn one's way in the world. When the card shows up as work, there is no value assessment attached in the way there was in the reading above. That said, there are jobs and there are jobs. All of us have had jobs where foxes lurked and perhaps pounced. But there is no need to assume this is the case. If a sitter asks you about their job or whether or not they will be hired for a certain job, the Fox (14) is simply the job itself. Period. It would be incorrect to assign any negative meaning to the Fox (14) in this case, unless, of course, the other cards in a spread were to lead you in that direction. For example, if a sitter asked if they would be hired for a new job and you drew Rider (1) / Fox (14) / Bouquet (9), then the spread indicates the sitter would be offered the job. On the other hand, you might well draw Rider (1) / Fox (14) / Snake (7). In this case, the news would probably not be what the sitter wants to hear. It would also perhaps be the case that it would be just as well the sitter did not get the job, because who knows what in the world is going on at that job with that Snake there?

If you were to draw a longer spread, with say, Rider (1) / Fox (14) / Scythe (10) / House (4) / Bouquet (9), it could be the case that the job would have already been earmarked for someone internal to the company, because Scythe (10) / House (4) implies *"Les jeux sont faites"* or the decision had already been made to hire someone internal to the company, probably as a promotion for a job well done (Bouquet 9).

You may still find all of these options confusing, but remember that I am providing you with hypothetical examples. Remember, too, that if you choose to read the way I do, Spirit / Higher Self / Source is your partner in the exercise as much as the cards are, and they will help you know where and how and why to ascribe meaning to specific card combinations.

CARD 15: BEAR

Bear

15

(*Mother, Financial Stability, Weight, Food, Appetite, Employer, Supervisor, Narcissist*)

The Bear (15) is another of my favorite cards because of the complexity it can present in a reading. Like Fox (14), Bear (15) can be perfectly benign, downright malignant, or something approaching neither of those extremes. Let us look at the various meanings and then see how Bear (15) might function in some small spreads that would make this point.

Above all, Bear (15) is the card for a maternal figure. Most of us have had such a figure in our lives, whether in the form of our own mother or grandmother, a favorite teacher, or an older neighbor. We know the archetypal vibe: warm, nurturing, consistent; a guide, a nurse, a cook, and a comforter. But, recall that physics assures us that for every action there is an equal and opposite reaction. There are mothers and there are mothers, am I right? Joan Crawford comes to mind . . . Bear (15) as mother can be as neglectful as she is careful, as cruel and controlling as she is kind. It all depends on the mother, the circumstances, and . . . the weather even, I suppose, because mothers are human beings who happen to have given birth or adopted or fostered or otherwise taken on responsibility for new life. Period. Motherhood does not, by definition, confer necessary sainthood upon any woman. So the archetype for Mother may be the idealistic, best version of motherhood, but *caveat emptor*. Assume nothing as to character when this card appears as mother, except that there is something fierce and unequivocal in her every position with respect to her offspring. It is she who is the bringer of life, and not the other way around. Think: "She who must be obeyed." Bear (15) is fierce in its opinions and unyielding in its possessiveness. Watch any Animal Planet show on bears and convince me that I am wrong. In any contest, Bear (15) will win, and sometimes the only option when in such a contest with a Bear (15) is to simply remove yourself from the action.

Bear (15) is a card of big appetites—for all kinds of things, not the least of which is food. Therefore, Bear (15) is the card for food, weight, and weight issues. If a sitter were to inquire about their health and Bear (15) were to pop up, then issues of diet would surely be part of the discussion. Generally, people who are overweight are well aware of their condition, so it is not as though you would be springing news on them to say that the cards suggest they look at their food choices in order to improve their health. Again, some readers make clear up front that they do not read on matters of health, so the whole subject could be something you would want to avoid. On the other hand, if you are open to exploring this issue with your sitter, you must be prepared to deal with matters of weight and diet with extreme sensitivity. A sitter may be avoidant or defensive, and if that happens, you certainly would not want to persist. The point will have been made by the Bear (15) card itself, and even if your sitter did not wish to discuss the matter with you, they would surely go home and ponder it in their heart. A Bear (15) always wins. Your sitter will have been given good information in order to make their own decision, in their own time, as to whether they or food itself will be the Bear (15) in that particular scenario. Your sitter could well decide to become the Bear (15) and exert control over their food choices. All you can do is show them what the cards have to say, and that is often all your sitter needs.

Speaking of winning, Bear (15) is also the card of financial success and stability. Bear (15) speaks to the kind of money that would be reaped from sound investments or inheritances. If paired with Clover

(2), this financial largesse would be the result of some unexpected windfall, but on its own, Bear (15) as a financial card implies either the need for, or the result of, careful planning and consistent growth of financial resources over time. One's major assets, such as homes and cars and stocks, would all come under this category. Often the money referred to by Bear (15) is not money that has been earned by the fruit of one's own labor. That is a different card, to which we will come in time. Bear (15) is about what one has actually done, or might want to consider doing, so that one's money grows from being simply the change in one's pocket to the consistent moving to the left of one's bank accounts' decimal points. Bear (15) is the card of money growth through sound investment.

In keeping with the theme of power and strength seen in Bear (15)'s role as either mother or financial stability, it should come as no surprise that Bear (15) is also the card for an employer, supervisor, or anyone who has say or sway about how you spend your time. A boss can be terrific or a terrific beast, or something else in between those two extremes, so it is important not to leap to any conclusion as to what type of boss Bear (15) might be referring to without a long look at the cards that surround Bear (15) when it shows up as a boss. Whip (11) / Bear (15) might imply that the boss in question could be quite the taskmaster, but then if one were to add on Bouquet (9) as a third card, it might bring the sense that this boss also appreciates the hard work of their employees and is apt to reward such industriousness. Many of us may have worked under such bosses, just as many of us may be acquainted with the tyrannical boss who is never satisfied and whose behavior borders on the abusive. Cards like Whip (11) and Bear (15) change when a third card is not Bouquet (9) or Clover (2), but rather something like Scythe (10), Snake (7), or Clouds (6).

This leads me to the last definition for Bear (15), which is as frequent in appearance as it is unpleasant to confront, and that is the Bear (15) as narcissist.

Now, of course a boss can be a narcissist; so can a mother. And there may be occasions where the Bear (15) will take on more than one role in a single reading. You will learn to see that the more you hone your skills. Frequently, though, the narcissist is neither boss nor mother, but simply someone in your sitter's life with certain traits that make interacting with them difficult. Sometimes, it can be your sitter themselves who show up as a narcissist. That's always lots of fun. Not.

Generally, when I see the Bear (15) as a narcissist, it shows up when a sitter asks about love. Most often, the sitter will ask about whether new love is coming in. Frequently when the Bear (15) shows up in a love reading, the sitter is currently or has recently been involved with a narcissist—someone who specializes in the fine art of gaslighting. The term is pretty common in the vernacular, but in case you are unfamiliar with it, here is a short overview: Gaslighting comes from the 1944 film *Gaslight*, starring Charles Boyer and Ingrid Bergman, who play a married couple. The dastardly husband wants his wife declared insane, because he murdered her famous aunt years before and does not want to be found out. He does things like steals her keys and makes her think she has misplaced them. Lights were lit by gas flame back then, and he keeps dimming the lights after she turns them up to make her think she doesn't know dim from bright. The entire time, he is solicitous and kind, assuring her he is only concerned for her welfare. It is all part of the mind game he is playing, and such behavior of first charm and then escalating efforts at manipulation and control are typical of the narcissist. In a love reading, when the Bear (15) appears early in the reading, I am frequently drawn to ask my sitter if they are or were previously involved with someone who behaved in certain narcissistic ways. The sitter will always confirm this, but frequently they will also add that the relationship is in the past, dealt with, over, finished. The thing is, though, that the presence of the Bear (15) in a past position in a reading about new love coming in tells me that this narcissist still has a hold on my sitter. When I suggest as much, the sitter will invariably say something like, "OMG! How did you know? They keep blowing up my phone and leaving long messages asking if we can get back together, apologizing for any hurt they caused. And when I say I have moved on, they get angry or sad, and then I feel bad and think about going back to them."

When this happens, I sit and listen, and then ask my sitter why that former flame has not been blocked from their phone, their social media, their mind? Invariably, I am met by silence. That is the type of hold the Bear (15) as narcissist can have on a person. And it is also the case that, until that Bear (15) is dispensed with by a wholesale and complete block, new love has no room to come into the sitter's life. And if new love were to come in before the narcissistic ex gets blocked in every way, it would probably be the same type of narcissistic energy that would be attracted and that would attract.

These are always hard conversations to have with sitters, but they are incredibly common. Narcissists don't have horns and tails that announce to us who they are. They walk among us. We all know them. Some of them know us, but we cannot tell who they are.

The primary thing to remember about the Bear (15) is that, whether mother or food issues, whether boss or finances or narcissist, the power the Bear wields is extraordinary. The cards can help a sitter navigate the choppy waters the Bear (15) can roil up. The Bear (15), like everything and like each one of us, does have its better angel side. Loving and nurturing, fierce in its protection, and grand in its scale, we only need to identify which Bear (15) we are dealing with, so that we know whether and how to approach. The Bear (15)'s Lenormand sister cards are always available to show that path.

• • •

Let's practice with the three cards we have just learned:

1. Child (13) / Fox (14) / Bear (15) = The child (Child 13) is keeping a sneaky (Fox 14) eye out for their mother (Bear 15). If we mirror

the cards Child (13) / Bear (15), we would also suspect that the mother is very well aware of the child's sneakiness. Also, Fox (14) and Bear (15) speak as much to the mother's all-knowingness as they do to the child's sneakiness.

OR:

_____

_____

_____

2. Fox (14) / Bear (15) / Child (13) = The detective (Fox 14) used his considerable resources (Bear 15) to track down new (Child 13) leads in the case.

OR:

_____

_____

_____

3. Bear (15) / Child (13) / Fox (14) =

_____

_____

_____

OR:

_____

_____

_____

CHAPTER 8

Stars (16) / Stork (17) / Dog (18)

CARD 16: STARS

(The Future, Hope, Evening, Internet, Rash, Pills, Metastasis)

Most often a positive card, Stars (16) in its broadest interpretation indicates the future. Of course, because the future includes all potential human experience, the card cannot automatically be ascribed a positive or a negative meaning. The surrounding cards in a spread will dictate that. The future is wide open, and the cards that appear together with Stars (16) can demonstrate just how much of a hand we can have in the shaping of ours. Therefore, it can feel like an encouraging card that reminds us that every single thing begins with a thought and that where we direct our thoughts will dictate much of our future. This is as true for the collective as it is for the individual. That is why Stars (16) is as much the card for hope as it is the card for the future.

Speaking of the future, something that I find charming and amusing is the fact that Stars (16) is also the card representing the internet and all things social media. Lenormand is a living language and must be viewed the same way we view, for example, the American Constitution: able to be interpreted in new ways to fit new circumstances. Surely the 19-century creators of this divination system did not foresee the invention of the internet, but how wonderful that there is a card that fits the definition perfectly. Stars are separate from each other and yet connected and visible in ways both intimate and informational. When lines are drawn between them, they form images that are at once familiar and comforting, as they are a reminder of the truth of "as above, so below." For example, the combination House (4) / Fox (14) / Stars (16) could indicate an online job one works from home.

In readings on love, Stars (16) can show up as internet dating. And for those who reel back in horror at the prospect, remember that internet dating is the updated version of sitting at a bar and having someone strike up a conversation with you by asking, "What's your sign?" It's better, though, right? Because you don't have to get up and leave the bar where you were enjoying yourself. With internet dating, with a single click that loser is lost. Poof! A reading where Stars (16) stands for internet dating can be very helpful in ascertaining how fruitful such an experience might turn out to be.

For questions of timing, Stars (16) is a card that indicates evening. So, for example, Stars (16) / Birds (12) / Clover (2) could indicate that you may have met someone interesting on the internet (Stars 16) whom you plan to meet up with (Birds 12) and that the evening (Stars 16) will be light and lots of fun (Clover 2). Not bad at all!

On a soberer note, Stars (16) can take a variety of meanings in readings on health. Sometimes an artist will portray only one star on the card, but more frequently, the Lenormand Stars (16) will show a galaxy of stars in a night sky. This puts one in mind of pills, which are small and come in multiples, so the card can reference medicine dispensed in such form. Stars sprinkled against a dark background also bring to mind a rash, particularly when appearing in a health reading with Clover (2), which will hint at something in the natural environment, such as poison ivy, that might be causing the rash. When appearing with the Bear (15) and seeming to be rash-related, it could well be that diet is the culprit for a rash. When appearing with, for example, Child (13) as well, the "diagnosis" could well be adolescent acne exacerbated by poor dietary choices.

While rashes and acne are always unpleasant, Stars (16)'s unpleasant side can be more difficult still, when it denotes cancer which has metastasized. I have seen this quite a few times in my years as a diviner. I am trained as a hospital chaplain and so have had considerable experience in being with people at difficult times. My heart always sinks a little when I see the Stars (16) as serious illness, but I also know how to address it. I will repeat the caveat I have given before to those of you unschooled in that way: it is perfectly fine to set parameters around what issues you will and will not read on. Legal issues and health issues should top any list of topics you may well want to avoid. But sitters will ask. It is critical that you let ethics and compassion act as your guides. You are neither lawyer nor doctor when you sit with someone as their diviner. That is something you should always make clear, and no sitter would fault you for taking a pass on questions better answered by those professionals.

Finally, and foremost, Stars (16) is a card of hope, forward movement, and grace freely given. Look to those meanings first, and let Stars (16)'s sister cards lead you down other paths, if that is where they tell you to go.

Stork

17

CARD 17: STORK

(Positive Change, Pregnancy)

One of the easiest cards in the Lenormand deck to make sense of is the
Stork (17). Nine times out of ten,
this card acts as the harbinger of swift
and positive change. Only occasionally, and for obvious reasons, will
Stork (17) refer to pregnancy, which
of course can be positive or negative
news, depending upon the perspec-
tive of the sitter. Generally speaking, Stork (17) is a card we should
be excited to see: if a spread indicates a good and happy situation, the
presence of Stork (17) assures that things will become even better.
If, on the other hand, a spread feels full of negativity, the presence
of Stork (17) is a signal that either this situation will undoubtedly
improve or that, however difficult the issue is at present, it is for a
greater good. For example, if we are prescribed a medicine that has
an awful taste, then the short-term experience (receiving the dosage)
is terrible, but the outcome (improved health) makes the overall situation better. There is no ambiguity about this card in the way that
there can be about our previous Stars (16) card. With the Stork (17),
help is on the way, things will get better, and whatever seems bad is
for a greater good that will shortly be made clear. Now, on to address
the Stork (17) as pregnancy.

Pregnancy is a life-changing event in every conceivable way.
Therefore, it is as serious as questions of illness, life and death, and
legal issues. If you are a novice reader, or even if you are a seasoned
reader but inexperienced with counseling others through circumstances that are troubling or traumatic, you may well want to add the

topic of pregnancy to the list of questions about which you will not read. There is absolutely no harm in choosing not to answer health, pregnancy, and legal questions. And there absolutely may be harm if you are unequipped to walk a competent, compassionate road with your sitter on these matters.

If you do choose to read on pregnancy, do not assume that every pregnant person will respond the same way to news that they are expecting. It is critical that you do not see the Stork (17) in a reading and then jump up and hug your sitter as you deliver to them the wonderful news. As always, the sister cards in the spread will give you a heads-up as to how your sitter might feel about the news that they are pregnant. Your job is not to assess value one way or the other. Also, you may be asked about a pregnancy that is very much wanted, only to see that there could be complications. An example of that might be Snake (7) / Stork (17) / Clover (2) / Scythe (10), indicating a problem (Snake 7) with the pregnancy (Stork 17) might require an emergency (Clover 2 for quick and unexpected) C-section (Scythe 10). I don't know that I would come out and say exactly that to a sitter. Instead, I would be quite serious about insisting that they keep all their doctor's appointments and stay closely monitored. Stork (17) / Snake (7) / Bear (15) / Lily (30) / Child (13) could indicate that there would be an issue with the pregnancy (Stork 17 / Snake 7) that would require the mother (Bear 15) remain on bed rest (Lily 30) for a portion of the pregnancy for the sake of the baby (Child 13). I hope I am being clear about what I mean when I say that pregnancy is a sensitive topic and ought to be read on only by those who are both seasoned and sensitive. We all like to think that as diviners, we are both of those things, but it is important that we all assess our own strengths and weaknesses and our ability to leave ego out of the equation for the sake of the sitter's highest good.

Dog

18

CARD 18: DOG

(Sibling, Cousin, Friend, Confidant, Nurse, Therapist, Counselor, Social Worker, Aide, Massage Therapist, Physical Therapist, Acupuncturist, Firefighter, Police, Loyal, Trustworthy)

As should be immediately clear from the keywords, if there were a spectrum of positive and negative in regard to Lenormand cards—and, as I have mentioned before, I think it is a bit simplistic to categorize them this way—there is no question that the Dog (18) would fall way to the positive side of that line. This means it finds itself at some distance on this imaginary spectrum from the Fox (14). If we were to go to a shelter seeking a pet and were offered the choice of a cute baby fox kit or an equally adorable puppy dog, chances are most of us would choose the puppy. The Fox (14), although frequently helpful in its own right, when it shows up as the medical specialist, scientist, or detective always has an agenda. Its primary intention is to ferret out information, to get to the bottom of something, and largely for its own self-interested reasons. The Dog (18), by definition, is different.

Think of the Dog (18) as sort of the comfort card of the deck, because in theory, this is a card that indicates a person or situation who/that is both supportive and safe. All by itself, Dog (18) is transparent, with no hidden agenda and no desire other than to be of help. But remember that one actually never reads a single Lenormand card by itself, right? Therefore, for all of Dog (18)'s positive attributes, the sister cards, which surround it in any given spread, are what will indicate the true nature of that particular Dog (18).

For example, one of the meanings of Dog (18) is sibling. Some of the absolute warmest relationships can be between siblings, who are, after all, our very first friends. But it is also the case, or so the Bible says, that Cain killed his brother Abel. Bad blood between siblings can be some of the worst blood imaginable. Whether a particular Dog (18) in a given spread is a best friend or a worst enemy will be indicated by the surrounding cards. And when the Fox (14) and the Dog (18) appear together in the same spread, what an interesting reading that can be! In life and in readings, it is critical to know the differences between these two.

I taught high school English for three decades. Very early in my career when chatting with a student, I asked him about his friends. With no emotional nuance at all, the student said to me,

Miss, I don't have friends. I have associates.

First, just so you know, my students insisted on calling me "Miss" when I was thirty and then still when I was sixty, so there's that. But also . . . as entirely taken aback as I was by this student's pronouncement, it was something I heard over and over again for the next thirty years. If you think about it, it makes some sense. School is where you go because it is where the adults say you have to go. You have no say in who your classmates are. All you may have in common with them is the fact that you live in the same district and perhaps you were born in the same year. Those facts, in and of themselves, do not friendships make. To these students, every other student was a Fox (14) until and unless they proved themselves to be a Dog (18). This is, of course, a cynical way to view the world, but teenagers are nothing if not cynical, as those who have raised them, taught them, or been them know. Another thing my students used to say was what I heard from my own mother: "Everyone who grins in your face is not your friend." So separating the Foxes (14) of your life from the Dogs (18) is a skill and an art that none of us can say we have perfected. Lenormand itself can be a Dog (18)-worthy ally that can help in the identification process during those times in your life when you are unsure.

Just as the Dog (18) is the card for siblings and friends, it is also the card for anyone in what are called the helping professions, as listed in the keywords above. Police are on the list, as their job description includes protection of and service to their community. I'll just leave that there for you to ponder.

• • •

Let's look at some examples of how our most recent three cards might appear in a three-card spread:

1. Stars (16) / Stork (17) / Dog (18) = This evening (Stars 16) there will be a mending (Stork 17) of a relationship with a friend (Dog 18).

    OR:

    _____

    _____

    _____

2. Stork (17) / Stars (16) / Dog (18) = Improvement (Stork 17) will come in the future (Stars 16) through working with a therapist (Dog 18).

    OR:

    _____

    _____

    _____

3. Dog (18) / Stars (16) / Stork (17) =

    _____

    _____

    _____

OR:

_____

_____

_____

CHAPTER 9

The Nine Box Spread

Now that we are through a second set of nine cards, it's time to look at how these cards might function in a Nine Box Spread. This spread is a traditional one and foundational for the ultimate spread you will learn later on, which incorporates all thirty-six cards. The Nine Box will call upon you to employ the skills you have already learned, such as reading lines of three and the mir roring technique we explored with lines of five and seven cards. You will also learn a new skill, called knighting, which will feel familiar to the chess players among you. The Nine Box Spread is always a fabulous fount of information, when approached carefully and slowly.

Here are the steps I follow in the order that I read a Nine Box Spread:

1. Identify the center card, as that will be the subject of the reading.

2. Look at the corner cards for context and theme.

3. Read the three-card vertical lines.

    a. The left line is past.

    b. The center line is present.

    c. The right line is future.

4. Read the three-card horizontal lines.

   a. The top line reflects thoughts.
   b. The center line reflects what is.
   c. The bottom line reflects hidden influences.

5. Read the two diagonal lines from top left to bottom right and then from bottom left to top right. These lines indicate movement and flow.

6. Mirror pairs of cards for more information. Remember that the only card that cannot be mirrored with another card is the card in the center of the spread, but that's not a problem. That center card is the subject of our reading. All other cards, whether pairs or trios, are filling in the details about that center card.

7. Knight cards to each other. This involves starting at any card and moving two cards up or down and then one card one over to get to a second card you will then assess along with the first. As in chess, any combination of two moves up or down followed by one over in either direction will bring you to your second card. Once you have your second card, you will essentially mirror them together, which only means coming to some conclusion about their interaction in light of the information you have gleaned from the rest of the reading. This is actually way less complicated than it sounds. It is also something I rarely do myself, as I have found that it merely corroborates what I have learned elsewhere in the spread. For my own Nine Box Spreads, I only ever do the first six steps, but I want you to have the option of adding on the seventh step if it is something that draws you.

So that you can see the Nine Box Spread in action, I will do one for you. For the sake of convenience, I will use the most recent cards you have learned, and I will put them in the order in which they were taught, but once you have studied that as your template, you should feel free to mix the cards up and come up with your own practice Nine Box for the eighteen cards you have in your repertoire so far. The combinations are not infinite, but certainly enough to provide some excellent practice on both the spread itself and in how groups of three cards can conceivably dance together. Remember that a Nine Box Spread is just several lines of three cards each.

Here is our spread. In this example, the cards are laid out 1 through 3 per each row. Normally, I would lay cards out for this spread in a Fibonacci sequence, which I will show you at the end of the book as a bonus tip. Laying the cards out that way feels like it adds to the magic, but it is not a requirement. Also, I will come up with a question once I see the cards laid out, because Lenormand loves working with specific questions.

NINE BOX USING CARDS 10-18

Scythe (10)	Whip (11)	Birds (12)
Child (13)	Fox (14)	Bear (15)
Stars (16)	Stork (17)	Dog (18)

Here, in order to form a question for us to work with, I will do what I would in any Nine Box Spread, which is to look first at the card in the center of our spread.

Wouldn't you know it would be the Fox (14)? Recall that the Fox (14) is the card for a medical expert, a person from a foreign land, a scientist, a detective, a suspicious person or a person whom we ourselves find suspect. This Fox (14) will not be all of these things, so it is our job as diviners to figure out what role the Fox (14) is playing here. Perhaps let that be our question then: What is this Fox (14) up to?

We will look to the corners first, as they provide context for the reading. I like to read clockwise, beginning with the top left card. Therefore, our corners for this spread will be read as Scythe (10) / Birds (12) / Dog (18) / Stars (16). The context for the question seems to be around a decision (Scythe 10) our Fox (14) will make related to networking (Birds 12) and friendship (Dog 18) so as to benefit their future (Stars 16).

The rest of the reading should confirm for us whether this is indeed the theme.

Next, we will want to look at the vertical lines, which begin here with Scythe (10) / Child (13) / Stars (16). Remember that this is total fiction, so I am just creating a story out of these combinations. The first part of the story, which we will call the past, or the backstory, tells us that a decision (Scythe 10) was made by this Fox (14) to try a little something new (Child 13) and see what might grow from it moving forward into the future (Stars 16).

Next, we move to the center vertical line, the one that holds our main character. This line, Whip (11) / Fox (14) / Stork (17), will tell us a bit about how the Fox (14)'s plan is working so far. It seems as though our Fox (14) is having to employ a considerable amount of discipline (Whip 11) in order to get a good result. In fact, our Fox (14) will have to step up their game if they want an even better result than they originally intended (Stork 17).

Now we will look at the last vertical line. It will let us know how this new project will work out for our Fox (14), with the cards Birds (12) / Bear (15) / Dog (18).

It looks like the project could well be a success, so long as our Fox (14) networks with (Birds 12) the right people who have both significant influence and the financial ability to fund the project (Bear 15) and will see the Fox (14) as trustworthy enough to invest in (Dog 18).

But there is far more to the Nine Box than just the vertical cards. Let's look next at the horizontal lines. The first one, comprised of the cards Scythe (10) / Whip (11) / Birds (12) identifies the thoughts the Fox (14) has about this project. It seems the Fox has indeed decided (Scythe 10) to buckle down (Whip 11) and make networking (Birds 12) a priority.

The second horizontal line takes thought and turns it into thing. It makes real what has heretofore been only a dream. The cards in this line are Child (13) / Fox (14) / Bear (15). It seems that, rather than hit up old contacts, the Fox (14) will need to establish a relationship with someone both new to them (Child 13) and powerful (Bear 15). On the other hand, the Fox (14) might also consider someone they may have known in childhood who has become successful and might be a willing investor. Remember that there are several entities involved in the reading of any spread: your sitter, the diviner, and the cards, which are the medium with which you work. If you choose to read as I do, Spirit, Higher Self, Source is also your partner. Recall that this spread is entirely made up. Were it a real spread for a real sitter and you were presented with the choice between the Fox (14) seeking out someone totally new and powerful or else someone they once knew when they were children, you would be given the right choice if you pay attention to Source with your intuition, your third eye, your third ear. That may feel to you like advice that is . . . impractical or not concrete. And yes, in my way of reading, that element is omnipresent and invaluable. It is your choice, always, whether to read in a concrete, journeyman way, or whether to let go and allow. I encourage the latter.

The final horizontal line lets us know the undercurrent of the situation. It gives us a glimpse into what the Fox (14) may not be aware of and ought to take into consideration if the project is to be a success. Here, those cards are Stars (16) / Stork (17) / Dog (18). What a perfect piece of advice this is for our self-interested Fox (14)! Our wily entrepreneur is being pulled up by the Universe and reminded that in order to have a good friend, one must first be a good friend. Whomever the Fox (14) approaches in regard to project investment must feel authenticity and genuine warmth from the Fox (14), and not just the pretense of it. In order to have a good future outcome (Stars 16), our Fox must dig deep inside (as this is the undercurrent horizontal line) in order to actually become a better (Stork 17), more genuine person (Dog 18). This self-improvement plan will pay far greater benefits than any conniving or scheming the Fox (14) might try instead.

Next, we can look at the diagonal lines of this Nine Box Spread. These lines identify movement and possibility, should the Fox (14) take the suggestions already outlined. First, let's look at the horizontal line formed by the cards Scythe (10) / Fox (14) / Dog (18). If this is a line of movement and possibility, we see that, indeed, our Fox (14) has within them the ability to make a conscious decision (Scythe 10) to move from guarded self-interest to trustworthy ally (Dog 18). That is good news indeed. The other horizontal line, Stars (16) / Fox (14) / Birds (12), implies that this project need not be a one-person operation and opens the possibility of partnership and networking (Birds 12) via social media (Stars 16) with potential partners in this enterprise. That is more good news for our Fox (14), who may have thought they had to go the road alone. Now our Fox (14) realizes otherwise.

The next thing one can do with a Nine Box Spread is to look at mirroring. If you recall, mirroring is simply looking at pairs of cards, instead of trios, and such pairing can serve to fill out any holes left in our reading. Often, mirroring provides confirmation of what we have already learned from our study of the lines of three. In a Nine Box, the center card, which acts as the subject of the reading, is the only card that cannot be mirrored with another card. So let's look at what cards we can mirror.

1. Scythe (10) mirrors Birds (12). Our Fox (14) has a decision (Scythe 10) to make regarding how to network (Birds 12).

2. Child (13) mirrors Bear (15), which identifies someone else of some financial standing, either new to the Fox (14) or else known to them from childhood.

3. Stars (16) mirrors Dog (18), indicating that our Fox (14) may want to check out and then contact this person via social media (Stars 16) in order to get the friendship/partnership (Dog 18) ball rolling.

4. Scythe (10) mirrors Stars (16), which definitely echoes the advice to decide (Scythe 10) on hitting up this potential benefactor on social media (Stars 16).

5. Whip (11) mirroring Stork (17) is confirmation of what we have already seen as advice to our Fox (14) to get organized and disciplined (Whip 11) if this project is to be successful (Stork 17).

6. Birds (12) mirroring Dog (18) reminds the Fox (14) that honey is the way to a bee's heart, and that the networking (Birds 12) they do must be authentic and sincere (Dog 18).

I hope you have noticed that nothing in this reading is contradictory to anything else in the reading. The cards act as confirmation, as caveat, as counsel. It is never Source's intention to obfuscate or to confuse, and I hope this reading has helped prove that point.

Finally, I will leave the knighting to you, except to tell you which cards knight with which cards in our spread so you can see how it works. It will, as I mentioned, prove confirmatory, but rarely provide you with novel information beyond what you've already learned from the previous steps. In this sample Nine Box I have shown you:

1. Scythe (10) knights to Bear (15) and Stork (17).

2. Child (13) knights to Dog (18) and Birds (12).

3. Stars (16) knights to Bear (15) and Whip (11).

4. Whip (11) knights to Dog (18) and Stars (16).

5. Fox (14) is the center card, our subject, and therefore cannot knight.

6. Stork (17) knights to Scythe (10) and Birds (12).

7. Birds (12) knights to Stork (17) and Child (13).

8. Bear (15) knights to Scythe (10) and Stars (16).

9. Dog (18) knights to Child (13) and Whip (11).

Just look at these cards and see if they give you any further information than what you already have. Maybe you will see something that I do not.

• • •

Now, on to the next set of cards. We are already halfway through the deck, and you have a strong base to see how the cards are already speaking volumes.

CHAPTER 10

Tower (19) / Garden (20) / Mountain (21)

CARD 19: TOWER

Tower

19

(Institution, School, Taxes, Law, Government, Authority, Office, Prison, Business, Hospital, Loneliness, Autonomy, Strength, Courage, Independence, The Spine and Back)

What a serious card this is. The Lenormand Tower (19) is always depicted as a stalwart, solid structure, impervious to storm or siege, cannon or cavalry. There is no arguing with the Tower (19), which is even more planted in power than the Bear (15). If it is indeed true that the only two sure things in life are death and taxes, the Tower (19) would be the second of that pair. This is the "She who must be obeyed" card. All things official come under the Tower (19), as does any building, edifice, or structure that is not

House (4). The Tower (19) is the card for backbone of both the literal and figurative variety, with all that this implies: courage, strength, implacability, imperviousness.

It is a good thing to have structures, entities, and personality traits that are dependable, strong, and predictable. But with Tower (19), that principle of physics again comes into play: the one that says that for every action, there is an equal and opposite reaction. A government entity, for all that it may be necessary, can be too stiff-necked and unyielding, not seeing the trees for the forest, not taking into account the individual in its focus on the collective. A person is able to stand upright thanks to a spinal column, and yet backs with spines that are too stiff cause inflexibility and pain. Just as independence and autonomy are admirable traits, inordinate cultivation of these same traits can result in isolation and loneliness. The Tower (19) can be as much prison as refuge. Which form it takes depends upon both circumstance and mindset, of course. In a card spread, whether the Tower (19) represents the one thing or the other is, as always, determined by the cards surrounding it. Depending on what cards the Tower (19) is combined with, this card can be comforting assurance or dire warning. If you come to the Lenormand Tower (19) from another system, such as Tarot, please know that the meanings of the Tower cards in these decks are diametric opposites of each other. The Lenormand Tower (19) will never catch fire, nor fall, nor cause any unfortunate falling of anyone from its great height. Often, in fact, Tower (19) is portrayed as a lighthouse, which makes the case for the occasions when this card acts as beacon, haven, hostel. The caveat, however, is that staying too long in the Tower (19) may initiate activation of its more sobering state.

To look at how the Tower (19) might function, take, for example, the five-card spread Tree (5) / Snake (7) / Bear (15) / Tower (19) / Scythe (10). Perhaps someone with stomach pain (Tree 5 / Snake 7 / Bear 15) will find themselves in the hospital (Tower 19) for a surgery

(Scythe 10). Or maybe someone will find themselves in prison for tax evasion: The big money of Bear (15) along with the evasion of Fox (14) leads to prison for tax stuff (Tower 19), with our card serving for both prison and tax.

In another example spread, let's look at:

Dog (18) / Whip (11) / Scythe (10) / Birds (12) / Garden (20) / Tower (19) / Coffin (8)

Perhaps friendly overtures (Dog 18) are so frequently rebuffed (Whip 11 / Scythe 10), that a person finds themselves socially (Birds 12 / Garden 20) ostracized (Tower 19), leading to a depression (Coffin 8) that was self-created. The possibilities are endless, but with patient practice and an opening of the senses, the sitter, the cards, Source, and your own connection to it will make context and message clear.

Garden

20

CARD 20: GARDEN

(Outside, Nature, Summer, Spring, The Public, Publicity, Party, Social Event, The Collective, Everyone)

The Lenormand Garden (20) is in many ways a card that is the opposite of both House (4) and Tower (19). In the case of House (4), that is because Garden (20) is the card that represents everything and everyone who is outside your front door. The moment you open the front door to House (4), all that lies before you is Garden (20). In the case of the Tower (19), with all its official and officious self-containment and autonomy—and sometimes, contrivance—the Garden (20) is all that is unconfined, uncontained, unpredictable, and natural. Now that we know what the Garden (20) is not, let us take a closer look at what it is.

The Garden (20) is public space, as in park or street or stage. And is it not the case that, whenever we walk out into the public, we are, in a sense, onstage? The Garden (20) is a reminder of the degree to which we are social beings, constantly both assessed and evaluated even as we assess and evaluate others. We long for connection, and we can be as broadened by it as we can be constricted by it. The Garden (20) dictates social mores and behavioral expectations. A walk in nature can provide us with delightful respite, and the Garden (20) would represent that, of course. But equally, the Garden (20) is comprised of those who would seek to box us into categories so they can wrap their minds around who they think we are or who they would like us to be. Therefore, depending on question, context, and sister cards, the Garden (20) can be beautiful and benign, land-mined with expectations of which we inevitably fall short, or all that lies in between.

Again, I am not of the belief that it is helpful to categorize each Lenormand card as good, bad, or neutral. I think that doing so, generally speaking, is a facile approach that takes into account neither the complexity inherent in each card nor the fact that single Lenormand cards act always in combination with others. It is the single card's Lenormand sisters that dictate the nature of that single card. Such, of course, is also the case for the Garden (20). Let's look at some three-card readings as examples:

Say a sitter is giving an outdoor party and asks you how it will go. Garden (20) is the card that would stand for the party. You might shuffle your deck, and then turn the cards over one at a time until you reach the Garden (20). Laying it in the center of your table, you would then place the card that appeared in the deck just before it to the left of it on the table. Then you would place the card that would have come after it to the Garden (20)'s right. This is now your line of three. Say that the line said:

Clouds (6) / Garden (20) / Snake (7)

This might indicate that bad weather (Clouds 6) would cause a problem (Snake 7). With this information in hand, your sitter could decide to move the party indoors. Now your sitter is prepared for such a contingency.

Or perhaps you would draw Birds (12) / Garden (20) / Bouquet (9), a reading which would indicate that the party would go smoothly to the degree that there would be lots of talking and connecting (Birds 12) that guests would enjoy and appreciate (Bouquet 9).

Let's look at a different question. Say your sitter asks how they might best address their depression. We will pull a seven-card spread this time and see where the Garden (20) might appear. This time, we will shuffle our deck and look for the Coffin (8), which is the card for depression:

Tower (19) / Clouds (6) / Ring (25) / Coffin (8) / Whip (11) /
Dog (18) / Garden (20)

Here, the depression is both caused by and exacerbated by social isolation (Tower 19). This has led the sitter to doubt themselves and whether they would be good company for anyone (Clouds 6). This thinking has a circular and cyclical aspect to it (Ring 25) which has caused the sitter to spiral into a depression (Coffin 8). The antidote to this would be for the sitter to take themselves in hand (Whip 11) and call a therapist, friend, or relative (Dog 18) to ask for help in finding their way back out into the world (Garden 20) again. Obviously this is a simplistic course of treatment for a serious problem, but you see how the cards can provide support to and confirmation for the sitter that the time is now to address this issue head-on.

Dog (18) / Whip (11) / Garden (20) could be something as simple as taking an actual walk (Whip 11) in the park (Garden 20) with an actual dog or a human friend (Dog 18). If you are working with intuition and Source as your partners for such a reading, you will know how to best interpret these cards for that particular sitter.

The Garden (20) is often a card of growth, expansion, and open-heartedness. Let the Garden (20)'s Lenormand sisters guide you in its interpretation, and you cannot put a foot wrong.

Mountain

21

CARD 21: MOUNTAIN

(Delay, Blockage, Pause, Obstacle, Hurdle)

The Lenormand Mountain (21) was a card I used to dread seeing when I was a novice reader. It made me immediately want to say, "Mountain, *Move!* Get out of the way!" Mountains are indeed impediments to progress. No one wants to be serenely striding down a predictable path, only to be stopped in their tracks by some seemingly insurmountable something. It is, at the very least, inconvenient, and it is often far more inhibiting. There is no misinterpreting the fact that, when presented with a Mountain (21), progress is stopped in its tracks. And there is no denying that the presence of the Mountain (21) in our lives can be disappointing, discouraging, or even infuriating. Over my many years of reading, however, both for myself and for thousands of others, I have learned to view the Mountain (21) differently. I am excited to share this with you, in the hopes that you will come to see this card as much a friend to you as all of her sister cards are, when in the right hands of the right reader with the right intention.

Two popular cultural—albeit dated—references come to mind when I see Mountain (21) in any reading. One is *The Sound of Music*, the 1965 film starring Christopher Plummer and Julie Andrews. It recounts the story of the Von Trapp family and their escape from Nazi-controlled Austria by car and on foot across the Alps, singing the whole way. What more formidable mountains can there be than the Alps? And yet, the family crossed over into safety. The other cultural reference is earlier still, but should nevertheless be familiar to many, and that is Walt Disney's animated characters in *Snow White and the Seven Dwarfs* of 1937. If you recall seeing this film as a child, you'll remember that the small men worked in a mine, digging for gems. While in real life that work would be backbreakingly difficult and dirty, these seven cheerfully wielded their pickaxes and their shovels. Remarkably, the gems they hewed from the mountain simply seemed to fly out of the gritty, forbidding rock that had held them. Miraculously, the gems emerged brightly colored, polished, and faceted. No wonder the little miners were so perpetually cheerful! Grumpy would have been far grumpier, I suspect, had the Mountain (21) not been so yielding of its colorful crop.

The lesson I learned from these two mountain stories was that not all obstacles are insurmountable, so long as we take the time to ponder their height and breadth and weight, and then assess our own abilities in how we might address them. The Lenormand Mountain (21) provides just such an opportunity to pause and reflect on any endeavor's next steps. Generally, when faced with the Mountain (21), our first instinct is to fall at the foot of it and put our heads in our hands in frustration, anger, or disappointment. That is not an inappropriate response; in fact, it is entirely human and to be expected. But such a response can't last forever. So what more might we do when faced with a Mountain (21) than rend our clothes and gnash our teeth because an obstacle has been thrown in our path?

What if we decide to climb the Mountain (21) in front of us? If we take the time the Mountain (21) demands, we can assess whether we have appropriate climbing gear. We can determine whether our fear of heights might preclude a quick and easy ascent. We may well decide to scale the Mountain (21) if we find ourselves both well-equipped and unafraid.

But the Mountain (21) asks that we wait a bit more. If we pause at the Mountain (21)—which is what it demands we do—we can take time to consider whether this Mountain (21) is an obstacle we can skirt by walking the long way around it. Lack of climbing equipment and fear of heights might make this an attractive alternative. But have we got food and a sleeping bag, since this approach, though easier, would take longer? Again, the Mountain (21) asks us to stop and reassess.

And as we sit still longer at the foot of that Mountain (21), wondering which should be our approach, we may decide to walk away and come back to it another day. Or, perhaps, if we gaze at the Mountain (21) long and hard enough, we may see that what had previously escaped our eye is the fact that there may well be daylight visible on Mountain (21)'s other side—a daylight that is accessible to us if we neither climb nor skirt around, nor walk away, but rather gather ourselves to walk right through that Mountain (21) toward the illumination that awaits us.

No one approach is best for every Mountain (21) we encounter. The point is that the Mountain (21) is not meant to disempower, but rather to do the opposite, providing us room and time to stop, reevaluate, and patiently ponder next steps. This makes the Lenormand Mountain (21) friend rather than foe, opportunity rather than impediment. In fact, every Lenormand card is a friend and opportunity, for together they warn, guide, and reassure. The Mountain (21) card is no exception.

Here is an example of a sitter question where Mountain (21) shows up so that you can see how an approach to such a question might look:

A sitter asks whether they will receive a raise at their current job, and you pull the following cards for a seven-card spread:

Fox (14) / Bouquet (9) / Snake (7) / Mountain (21) / Clover (2) / Ship (3) / Stork (17)

This could be read to say that the job (Fox 14) promotion (Bouquet 9) is not immediately forthcoming (Mountain 21) due to some sort of professional sabotage or perhaps just red tape (Snake 7), but this is actually a lucky break (Clover 2) because it causes the sitter to say that enough is enough and look elsewhere for employment that will present them with more and better opportunities (Ship 3 / Stork 17). Perhaps, had that Mountain (21) not been there, the sitter would have stayed at that original place of employment and been stuck in a dead-end job. Sometimes gifts come disguised as disappointments. Just as often, the Universe has a plan even better than the one of which we could conceive. The Mountain (21) gives us time to recognize that and respond accordingly.

• • •

Now that we have learned three more cards, let's look at them in combination with each other to see what stories they might tell.

1. Tower (19) / Garden (20) / Mountain (21) = Feeling lonely (Tower 19) even in the midst of a crowd (Garden 20) is a state of mind that ought to give one pause (Mountain 21) as it is an issue worth addressing.

   OR:

   _____

   _____

   _____

2. Garden (20) / Mountain (21) / Tower (19) = Ascribing to groupthink and a herd mentality (Garden 20) can be an impediment (Mountain 21) to finding one's own sense of autonomy (Tower 19).

   OR:

   _____

   _____

   _____

3. Mountain (21) / Tower (19) / Garden (20) = Taking a few deep breaths and perhaps meditating for a bit (Mountain 21) would help you compose and center yourself (Tower 19) before going into that crowded arena to perform (Garden 20).

   OR:

   _____

   _____

   _____

CHAPTER 11

Crossroads (22) / Mice (23) / Heart (24)

CARD 22: CROSSROADS

(Choices, Alternative Health, Twins, Part-Time Job, Dual Role, Coronary Arteries)

The first order of business in our discussion of the Crossroads (22) is to make the distinction between it and the Scythe (10). Crossroads (22) is the card for choices. Even in its singular form of *choice* that word implies at least two options from which a single one will be selected. Scythe (10) is that single decision. The Scythe (10) is the result of the contemplation of the Crossroads (22). In fact, if you think of the Scythe (10) as singular and of the Crossroads (22) as plural, you will never run the risk that some diviners do, of confusing the cards with each other.

Usually depicted as a central point from which several roads extend like spokes on a wagon wheel, the Crossroads (22) reminds us that we are never as stuck as the Mountain (21), which is the previous card, might have us think. It is a good and a right thing to stand at the center of that wagon wheel, which is the place where the roads all converge and cross, before making any Scythe (10)-like decision. The Crossroads (22) is the card that assures us there are choices before us. It also assures us that even when we pick a road, we need only walk far enough down it to discern whether it is the right one for us in the moment or not. We are always free to recalibrate, to do a cost-benefit analysis, to change our minds and double back to the center and, from there, choose another path. Crossroads (22) reminds us that life—and therefore the Lenormand, which tells the story of our lives—is both malleable and mutable. There is no shame or harm in answering a soul call to change course midstream and go a new and different way. In fact, if you live long enough, you will discover that failure to heed such a call from the soul will result in the change being made *for* you, often in ways you will find inconvenient at the least and downright difficult at the other end of the spectrum. Crossroads (22) is a call to arms to take charge of our lives to find our path—and to recognize it only for as long as it feels like our path. When it no longer feels right, Crossroads (22) is the call to arms to go another way. We are presented with Crossroads (22)-type choices every day, in every moment. That fact can be as liberating as it can be daunting. And in those times when it is daunting, the sister cards that show up with Crossroads (22) are there to suggest new paths.

In a reading on work matters, the Crossroads (22) can refer to work that is part-time or a passion project side gig. In matters of health, the Crossroads (22) can be suggestive of alternative health approaches, such as yoga, acupuncture, massage, or meditation, being potentially beneficial and as an adjunct to any Western medicine treatment plan the sitter may be taking. In a reading on pregnancy (and

I suggest you go back and read what I have to say about pregnancy readings in my discussion of Stork 17), Crossroads (22) hints at the possibility of twins or multiples. Also, in a pregnancy reading, Crossroads (22) may speak to alternate ways of achieving parenthood that extend beyond personal pregnancy, such as surrogacy, fostering, and adopting. Finally, in regard to health, when Crossroads (22) appears with the Heart (24) and the Mountain (21), a coronary artery blockage could be an issue. Again, I enjoin you to refrain from readings on health, legal matters, or pregnancy unless you are skilled in more than the reading of cards to address such issues.

The primary message of the Crossroads (22) for me is always the fact that life is fluid when we are flexible. How and when and whether we exercise such flexibility will be elaborated on by the sister cards that appear when the Crossroads (22) takes center stage in a reading. This is a card of opportunity and options, rather than perplexing indecision, when read together with other cards in the context of a well-phrased question.

Mice

23

CARD 23: THE MICE

(Anxiety, Fear, Stress, Excitement, Erosion, Decrease, Dirt, Disease)

The Lenormand Mice (23) have been a remarkable example to me in the ways card meanings can morph and expand for a diviner over time and with much practice. First, though, I will discuss how the card has been traditionally interpreted. Mice (23) are small, quick creatures who love to scurry about and nibble at things. They are commonly considered vermin and therefore are unwelcome signs of disorder, uncleanliness, and disease, of which, after all, they are notorious carriers. Tree (5) / Mice (23) / Bear (15), for example, would put me in mind of some sort of foodborne illness (with Tree 5 for health and Bear 15 for food) caused by poor sanitation (with Mice 23 for both illness and poor sanitation).

Because they are noted gnawers, when the Mice (23) appears, the energy of whatever card comes before it in a spread will be eroded, diminished. If one were to receive a gift of some sort (Bouquet 9), and the Mice (23) followed, the magnitude or the quality of the gift or the spirit in which such a gift was given would be somehow lessened. For example, if you were to unwrap a gift and find that it was a candle, that would be lovely, until you noticed that the candle had already been burned down and was therefore not a gift, but a "regift" from someone who did not care at all whether or not you would notice that the candle had already been used. That would be Bouquet (9) / Mice (23). Of course, I am not saying I am against regifting. I just think if one is going to do it, it ought to be thoughtfully executed. There is something disrespectful about Bouquet (9) / Mice (23), particularly if we add an extra card like Fox (14) or Snake (7) to the three-card spread. Either of those cards would imply that whoever gifted the used candle actually wanted the recipient to feel slighted.

In keeping with this idea of Mice (23) being detractors, let's say we asked about whether a trip would go well. If we got the cards Ship (3) (trip) / Mice (23) (cut short) / Clouds (6) (bad weather), we would deduce that the trip would be called off or cut short because of inclement weather. If we wanted to learn in what kind of mood we might be by day's end, and we saw Stars (16) / Sun (31) / Mice (23) / Clouds (6) / Coffin (8), we might anticipate that, by evening (Stars 16), our pleasant disposition (Sun 31) would have been eroded (Mice 23) to the point where we would be confused (Clouds 6) and exhausted (Coffin 8).

Over time, as I mentioned in the beginning of my treatment of the Mice (23), I have come to see them as sometimes the opposite of all such negative meaning. As a cultural reference, I point you to another Disney classic cartoon, *Cinderella*. (Can you tell I am a child of the 1960s?) In that fairy tale, as we all know, the poor, orphaned Cinderella exists only at the mercy of her merciless stepmother and stepsisters. Long story short, she wants to go to the Prince's ball, but has no wherewithal to get there and certainly not to arrive appropriately coifed and clothed. As you recall, if you've seen the film, Cinderella's only friends are the mice infesting the otherwise stately home which she cleans "from can't see in the morning until can't see at night," as my mother would have said. These mice, true to form, are frenetic and frantic, scurrying and nibbling in a mouselike manner. But they are also Cinderella's friends, and when all of their anxious, nervous (Mice 23) energy is harnessed for the purpose of making Cinderella's ball experience a memorable one, they prove to be imaginative, industrious, and intent on following through on all their self-assigned tasks. With the help of Cinderella's fairy godmother, these mice turn rags into *haute couture* and a pumpkin into a coach. In Lenormand, the Mice (23) frequently appear for me as eagerness, excitement, enthusiasm, especially with the lucky Clover (2) card.

Mice (23) / Clover (2) / Bouquet (9) feels a little like the Christmas morning hyped-up vibe of children ready to see what Santa might have left for them under the tree. You will be asking me why I would not interpret this Mice (23) card as detracting from such early morning joy, because, after all, the Mice (23) is a detractor and a nibbler and gnawer-away at good things. If these are the only cards in this spread, I would be inclined to stick to my interpretation, as the Bouquet (9) is a beautiful card with which to end a spread. But if I got a sense that there might be more to the story, I would simply pull another card or two to either confirm or dispel my initial sense of things. If I were to pull two more cards and the whole spread read

Mice (23) / Clover (2) / Bouquet (9) / Clouds (6) / Snake (7), then yes, I would say that chances are that the Grinch will have indeed stolen Christmas, with the Mice (23) as his dastardly assistants. But if the two clarifying cards I pulled caused the line to be Mice (23) / Clover (2) / Bouquet (9) / Child (13) / Stars (16), I would say that in that house on that Christmas morning joy reigned supreme, because the children of that household had received the gifts on their wish lists, with not a preburned candle among them.

So, when you are trying to determine whether the Mice (23) are friend or foe, excitement or woe, my advice is as it has ever been: look to the sister cards and your own intuition.

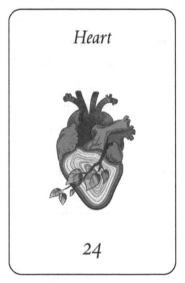

Heart

24

CARD 24: HEART

(Love, Romance, Anatomical Heart)

Must one really explain the Heart (24)? The Lenormand Heart (24) is that universal symbol for love, of course, and so, in theory, we already know what that means. Whether the love spoken of in a particular card spread is filial or agape, romantic or altruistic, or some other kind entirely, is dependent, as you already also know, on the accompanying cards. Also, when the card refers to the actual anatomical heart, there are card combinations which are worth exploring. Therefore, it might be best to just jump into some two-card and then three-card combinations with cards we have already learned. Let's look at what the cards might have to say about both the anatomical organ, whose beating keeps us breathing, and how that same symbol functions as the representation of love, the thing we alternately all understand and at the same time find utterly incomprehensible.

In a health reading (and remember, it is fine to decide not to do health readings if you do not feel adequately equipped), when the Heart (24) shows up, the presenting issue may be anatomical, but it could just as easily be emotional in nature. Heartbreak itself can be both literal and figurative, can it not? If you are someone who does choose to do health readings, do not immediately leap to any conclusions when you see the Heart (24). Listen to the sister cards, and to what Spirit whispers in your third ear. Here is a sample reading:

Tree (5) / Whip (11) / Heart (24) / Tower (19) / Scythe (10)

This series might indicate a couple of things. If the problem were physical in nature and the cards showed up like this, one might read that there was a health issue (Tree 5) of a painful variety (Whip 11), which did or would result in a hospital stay (Tower 19) and a surgical procedure (Scythe 10). But what if the issue were to be psycho-emotional, rather than physical? Those same cards might be read this way: The querent feels emotionally beaten up (Tree 5 / Whip 11) because their heart (Heart 24) is lonely (Tower 19) and broken (Scythe 10).

You see how critical it is that you pause and listen to Spirit and your intuition before opening your mouth to do any reading? While these two experiences may, each in their own way, feel agonizingly painful, they are very different ones. As a diviner, it is important that you not mistake the one experience for the other. Disciplined study, a willingness to listen to your intuition, and experience of reading for wide swaths of people are what will help you know the difference.

A lighter-hearted spread (pardon the pun) might be something like this:

Bear (15) / Scythe (10) / Clover (2) / Child (13) / Heart (24) / Bouquet (9) / Dog (18)

This might be read as:

The mother (Bear 15) decided (Scythe 10) to surprise (Clover 2) her child (Child 13) by fulfilling their heart's desire (Heart 24) and giving them (Bouquet 9) the Dog (Dog 18) they had wanted for so long.

As you can see, a heart is a heart is a heart. The only way we can know if it beats or breaks or swells with emotion is by using our diviner's skill to learn the steps of the sister cards who dance with the Heart (24) differently for each sitter and each sitter's question.

• • •

Now, using the three most recent cards we have learned, let's see how they might work in combination with each other.

1. Crossroads (22) / Mice (23) / Heart (24) = Having more than one choice (Crossroads 22) in the situation, the sitter narrowed them down (Mice 23) and went with the one that called to her heart (Heart 24).

    OR:

    _____

    _____

    _____

2. Mice (23) / Heart (24) / Crossroads (22) = The sitter is anxious (Mice 23) about a heart condition that will possibly require a coronary bypass (Heart 24 / Crossroads 22).

    OR:

    _____

    _____

    _____

3. Heart (24) / Crossroads (22) / Mice (23) =

_____

_____

_____

OR:

_____

_____

_____

CHAPTER 12

Ring (25) / Book (26) / Letter (27)

CARD 25: RING

(Commitment, Contract, Marriage, Ring, Promise, Permanence, Eternity, Cycle, Wheel, Circular, Perennial, Season, Chronic)

The Lenormand Ring (25) is the card for all things circular or cyclical in nature. If you were to be asked about the timing of an event, for example, you could decide in advance of pulling your cards whether you want the Ring (25) to represent a week, a month, or a year. All divining methods are notoriously inaccurate as to timing, because divining is the act of moving information from the dimension which my mother would call "the fullness of time," or kairos, to chronos, or time on the watch, the clock, the calendar. Certain cards can be helpful, though, in trying to at least approximate a time frame. The Tree (5), for example, stands for a long time, such as a year or more. Clover (2) stands for a brief time, ranging from moments to minutes to days. The Ring (25) refers to time as it presents itself in its cyclical form; hence it is my card to represent all the seasons. It is the card for contracts that are binding, such as mortgages or marriages. Was anyone here a Girl Scout? I was not, but I know the song they sing:

A circle is round; it has no end, and that's how long I want to be your friend.

There is also the old country hymn sung at funerals that asks the mournful question:

Will the circle be unbroken by and by, Lord? By and By? There's a better home a-waiting, in the sky, Lord, in the sky.

Human beings seem to find the roundness of circles satisfying. Perhaps they make us think of the prehistoric campfire circles we huddled around for warmth and companionship. We learned to tell the same stories over and over at campfire after campfire, as the Greeks echoed later on in history with their plays that people knew by heart but returned to circular amphitheaters to watch over and over again, for the sake of the cathartic release they provided. The Ring (25) is the card for the vows we make and the promises we keep: it is the card for all that we cherish for its permanence in our lives. It is the card for eternity. For example, if a sitter were to ask you about new love coming in—probably the most common question any diviner will hear—and the card pull were Bouquet (9) / Heart (24) / Ring (25), then the reading would indicate that this love would prove to be true and enduring.

But remember that for every up, there is a down, and the Ring (25) card is no exception to this principle of physics. If a sitter were to ask you about the state of their marriage and you pulled Fox (14) / Ring (25) / Scythe (10), you might get an inkling that someone in that marriage was potentially being dishonest (Fox 14) and that such betrayal might result in the marriage (Ring 25) breaking up (Scythe 10).

Anything that is binding has the potential to be constricting, and therefore unhelpful and unhealthy. For example, in a health reading, if one were to draw a three-card spread of Tree (5) / Clouds (6) / Ring (25), one might wonder if the issue had to do with circular thinking. If the spread were augmented by two other cards so that it now read Tree (5) / Clouds (6) / Ring (25) / Whip (11) / Coffin (8), one might wonder if the sitter were dealing with a health issue (Tree 5) of an emotional nature, such that their negative thoughts (Clouds 6) were circular (Ring 25) and incessantly punishing (Whip 11), resulting in depression (Coffin 8). If this is what you saw in your cards, you, of course, would suggest your sitter seek the support of a mental health professional. Any sort of obsessive-compulsive behavior would be indicated by such cards. Circular thinking occurs in even the most emotionally and mentally healthy among us. Lenormand is a wonderful oracle to help those caught in such a vise to find the pressure-release valve so they can move forward, but again, Lenormand is not a substitute for professional medical help. In a reading on physical health, the Ring (25) could indicate a problem of a chronic—as opposed to acute—nature. For example, the flu is an acute illness, in that, however unpleasant it may be, it has both a point of onset and an ending. An example of something chronic would be seasonal allergies, which should always be suspected in a health reading if Clover (2) and Whip (11) appear with Ring (25).

All of that said, the Ring (25) is generally a lovely card, portending security and permanence, particularly when paired with cards that support that idea. As always, let the qualities of the Ring (25) be told to you by her sister cards. They will always let you know whether that circle is the coveted brass ring, the dreaded noose, or something in between.

Book

26

CARD 26: BOOK

(Secrets, The Unknown and Unknowable, Undiscovered, Actual Book)

The Lenormand Book (26) is quite a conundrum of a card. On the one hand, we know that books are literally written words on pages that are held together by a cover. We know books as sources of knowledge, enlightenment, and entertainment. Books are where we go for guidance or to be roller-coaster-style terrified from the comfort of an easy chair. Books comfort and teach. Sometimes, in a given spread, the Lenormand Book (26) card can do all of those things.

Here is a plot twist, though: as common as that understanding may be of what the function of an actual book is in our lived contexts, the Lenormand Book (26), far more often than not, is a signal that there is a secret kept, information hidden, or an unforeseen circumstance which has yet to unfold. It is the card for mystery, intrigue, or simply downright ignorance. Whoever decided to ascribe such meaning to the Book (26) deserves a nod for a naughty sense of irony. How can the Book (26) possibly stand for all we have been given to understand is its opposite? I have no answer to that question. I am just teaching you the rules. But as you also know by now, rules—once understood and practiced—can certainly be bent and shaped to suit other ends. Keep that in the back of your mind for a moment.

Some deck creators, when making the Book (26) card, will choose to portray an open book, while other artists portray the Book (26) as closed. Therefore, there are readers who will decide that if they are working with a deck with a Book (26) card that is open, they will interpret that Book (26) in the way that is commonly, historically, traditionally understood. That is to say, they will consider that card as representative of knowledge known, information understood, awareness awakened. From my perspective, that is another Taroistic interpretation of a Lenormand card, because it is dependent on the artist's caprice to have drawn the book as open. That is not in keeping with the original Lenormand meaning of the Book (26). Therefore, I would never interpret the Book (26) as information learned or uncovered without other corroborative cards in the spread that would confirm such an interpretation. For me, the Lenormand Book (26), whether depicted as open or closed, is the card of secrets, information hidden, knowledge either undiscovered or undiscoverable. This undiscovered information, by the way, need not be nefarious in nature, although it sometimes is. Again, whether we are seeing a surprise party in the works—Bouquet (9) / Book (26) / Garden (20)—or whether we are seeing a cheating spouse on the horizon—Ring (25) / Fox (14) / Book (26) / Heart (24) / Snake (7)—depends on the sister cards surrounding the Book (26).

Sometimes, a Book (26) is just a book, as could be the case when, for example, your sitter asks about a book they have written and its prospects for success in the marketplace. If the cards Book (26) / Rider (1) / Birds (12) / Bear (15) were to turn up, that would be auspicious financial (Bear 15) news (Rider 1) in regard to the success of this actual, physical book, about which a lot of buzz (Birds 12) would have been generated.

I mentioned that some diviners want the Lenormand Book (26) to only, always, and ever represent an actual book or information revealed or known. It is possible to set that intention for that card, but then it is important that you be consistent in your interpretation so as not to confuse yourself. A far better course of action, I think, is to let the sister cards dictate the role the Book (26) is taking in a particular spread.

Finally, the Book (26) can often represent information that is simply unknowable in the moment. For example, a sitter might want to ask you if they will die from a particular illness, pass a particular test, meet the perfect lover. When the Book (26) appears in such a spread—and depending on how and where the Book (26) appears—the reading may indicate that other things need to play out first before such information can be gleaned. In the case of the person asking about passing a test, for example, if they do not intend to study for the test, the results could go one way. If they apply themselves and burn the midnight oil, the results could go another. Human beings have agency in their lives. Whether or not they choose to exercise it is a different question entirely. However, when the Book (26) appears in such a reading, it is acting as a gentle reminder to your sitter to take the helm in the ways that they can and do their part to steer the situation in the direction they would like it to go, whether that is seeking out a second opinion and following doctor's recommendations in the case of the illness question, studying in the case of the exam question, and being clear about both what they want and what they have to offer, when it comes to questions about love. The Book (26) is an invitation to participate in our own lives so that we are the ones who write that story in our own Book of Life.

The Language of Lenormand

Letter

27

CARD 27: LETTER

(Diploma, Receipt, Bill, Thank-You Note, Get Well Card)

The Lenormand Letter (27) is a card that can be explained the most quickly, and it is simultaneously possibly the most unsatisfying of all the cards in the deck. The Lenormand Letter (27) stands for anything at all in written form. How's that for being vague and specific at the same time? The Letter (27) could be an actual letter. It could also be a recipe, a report card, a prescription, a parking ticket, or an electricity bill. It can be a greeting card, a newspaper article, an eviction notice, or a cum laude diploma. The Letter (27) can even be a blank sheet of paper just waiting to be written upon. As frustrating as such vagueness is, there is hope in the fact that, as always, the nature and meaning of the Lenormand Letter (27) are revealed by its interaction with its sister cards. For example, an invitation to a party to be held in the evening might be Letter (27) / Garden (20) / Stars (16). A summons to court for a traffic ticket might be something like Letter (27) (summons) / Tower (19) (to court) / Ship (3) (for a traffic infraction). If you allow yourself to lean first on the Letter (27)'s supportive sisters, then you will be far less inclined to pull an answer from thin air or your own imagination.

• • •

Now, let's look at some three-card combinations with the last three cards we've covered.

1. Ring (25) / Book (26) / Letter (27) = Whether he would ask her to marry him (Ring 25) remained up in the air (Book 26) until she received a letter (Letter 27) from him telling her of his intentions.

   OR:

   _____

   _____

   _____

2. Book (26) / Letter (27) / Ring (25) = The sitter cannot find (Book 26) the important document (Letter 27) although they have looked for it repeatedly (Ring 25).

   OR:

   _____

   _____

   _____

3. Letter (27) / Ring (25) / Book (26) =

   _____

   _____

   _____

   OR:

   _____

   _____

   _____

CHAPTER 13

Nine Box for Cards 19–27

Now that we have learned our third set of nine cards, it is time to see how these most recent cards, 19–27, might read in a Nine Box Spread. I have shuffled just these nine cards and will draw the spread randomly, letting the Universe assign the subject and the message pertaining to it. Here are the cards as I have drawn them:

Ring (25)	Heart (24)	Book (26)
Mountain (21)	Garden (20)	Mice (23)
Letter (27)	Tower (19)	Crossroads (22)

As with our other example, I will now work through the same six steps I always use to read this spread:

1. Center Card: The very first thing I look at in a Nine Box Spread is the center card, because that will immediately tell me the subject of the reading. If this were an actual reading for a real sitter and they had a question on a specific area, I would be most inclined to preselect that center card to represent that area. I might not, though. Sometimes, even when you want to look at a particular area, it can be fascinating to see the perspective from which the cards might encourage you to view that subject by just letting the deck decide what that center card should be. It can help shift your viewpoint in amazing ways. Here, in our reading for an imaginary sitter, we have done just that: allowed the deck to determine the subject, which, as we see is the Garden (20). Recall that the Garden (20) stands for anything to do with outside, nature, the public, other people, parties, even performances. We do not know which of these things our cards will address, but we are about to find out. Out of an infinite number of subjects upon which the cards might conceivably focus, we have automatically narrowed things down to only the meanings ascribed to the Garden (20). With just that card, we have made great headway.

2. Next, we look at the four corners of the spread, going clockwise from the top left card, in order to ascertain the theme of the spread, which we already know has to do with some attribute of the Garden (20). Our corners for this spread are Ring (25) / Book (26) / Crossroads (22) / Letter (27). It seems that the theme of the reading will be whether or not (Book 26 / Crossroads 22) to

commit to something in writing (Letter 27). Because we are dealing with the Garden (20) as our subject, this commitment would
be of a public nature, as perhaps a wedding would be, where rings
are exchanged and signatures are affixed to a certificate (Ring 25
/ Letter 27). But there are many circumstances where promises
are made and signed off on in a public way. Anything notarized,
for example, has a signature that is witnessed by someone who
counts as Garden (20). We will find more specificity as we move
along further in the spread.

3.   Next, it is time to evaluate the vertical lines. As you recall, we can
     look at these lines in terms of past, present, and future. The line
     representing events that have already transpired is comprised of
     Ring (25) / Mountain (21) / Letter (27). It seems that this public
     declaration of commitment has been previously delayed. Perhaps
     a reluctant bride or groom had been dragging their feet. Or per-
     haps, as in the case of a contract of some other kind, there had
     been some sort of holdup on the paperwork, delaying effectuat-
     ing this contract. The second vertical line speaks to the situation
     as it currently stands. We have Heart (24) / Garden (20) / Tower
     (19). This indicates that the contract in question may well have to
     do with love (Heart 24) and that the issue is whether this love will
     be made official (Tower 19) in the eyes of the community (Gar-
     den 20). The third vertical line addresses how this situation will
     turn out, with Book (26) / Mice (23) / Crossroads (22). Uh-oh. It
     seems as though whoever is in possession of those cold feet (Mice
     23) will be remaining clueless (Book 26) as to how to choose
     (Crossroads 22) whether to commit or not.

4.   The next order of business is to consider the horizontal lines. The
     top line indicates what our person is thinking: Ring (25) / Heart
     (24) / Book (26). These cards confirm that whether they love the
     other person enough to make this commitment (Ring 25 / Heart

24) is kind of up in the air (Book 26). I remind you that the center horizontal line is the one that turns thoughts into things, and here, we have Mountain (21) / Garden (20) / Mice (23). It looks like, regardless of whether the wedding has been paid for and the guests are in their seats, someone will indeed be left bereft at the altar. The Mountain (21) blocks the social event (Garden 20) from moving forward because of last minute jitters (Mice 23). The final horizontal line hints at the situation's undercurrent: Letter (27) / Tower (19) / Crossroads (22). With the signing of a marriage certificate, the reluctant partner realizes that things would be official (Tower 19) and they would have crossed a number of roads off in terms of future choices they might otherwise be able to make for themselves (Crossroads 22).

5. The diagonal lines speak always to movement and possibility. Ring (25) / Garden (20) / Crossroads (22) indicate that the wedding proceeding at a later date could indeed be a possibility. Letter (27) / Garden (20) / Book (26), however, mean that that marriage certificate will not be signed today.

6. Finally we can mirror certain cards to check our work on this spread. In a Nine Box Spread, the only card that cannot be mirrored with another card is the center card, which, in this case, is the Garden (20). We can mirror Ring (25) with Book (26) to confirm that this marriage (Ring 25) moving forward is far from certain (Book 26). We mirror Heart (24) and Tower (19) and learn that the person who is holding back may well feel all alone and friendless (Tower 19) in making this choice to back out. Book (26) mirrors Crossroads (22) to say that this person really has no idea what path to take. Mountain (21) mirrors Mice (23), confirming the fact that anxiety is holding things up. Letter (27) mirrors Crossroads (22), which is simply more corroboration that the reluctant one needs to weigh pros and cons before proceeding.

Notice that nothing has contradicted what our initial thoughts were when we looked at the four corners of this spread in the very beginning. The Nine Box is an extremely satisfying spread because if you don't immediately catch something with one glance, you will surely find it elsewhere in the spread and be able to confirm it in myriad ways. I am sorry for all those imaginary guests and for the imaginary prospective bride and groom at this imaginary wedding, but as always, I am grateful to the cards for helping to draw us so clear a picture of the Wedding That Wasn't!

Finally, if you decide you want to triple-check your work, you can go through the extra step of seeing which cards knight other cards as I showed you how to do in the first Nine Box Spread we reviewed. I do not do this triple check, because it feels redundant, but if you are a novice reader, knighting will give you just that much more confidence that you have read the spread with pinpoint accuracy.

CHAPTER 14

Man (28) / Woman (29) / Lily (30)

CARD 28: MAN

(Man, Male Querent or Subject, Masculine, Aggressive, Assertive, Yang Energy)

The next two cards will go quickly for us in terms of ferreting out their meaning. If your sitter identifies as male, this will be the card representing him. If your sitter is of either or any gender and is inquiring about a man, this would be the card you would focus on

in your reading, as everything you see would revolve around him and his thoughts, feelings, and actions. I am sure that needs no elaboration. What may, however, need some explication is that sometimes, when the Man (28) appears in a reading, the card is not referring to an actual male person at all, but to the kind of energy we culturally and stereotypically associate with a man. That is to say, assertive, hard-charging, definitive, and decisive. There are plenty of men who were not endowed with such characteristics in copious quantities, which is probably all to the good. But understand that, when you are doing a reading and there is no actual man in the picture, on the horizon, at the table, or in question, then it is a good idea to think of the card as representing something energetic as opposed to someone actual. There are absolutely times in our lives when, regardless of the gender we were assigned or the gender with which we identify, we need to pull from the recesses where our resources reside an assertiveness, a self-assurance, a confidence and willingness to act. All of this is inherent in the Man (28). Lenormand was created in a certain era and a certain cultural context, and so some may find offensive the very idea of a Man (28) card as representative of the above characteristics. I am acknowledging that, and then suggesting that, for the purposes of making Lenormand an oracle that works for us, we move on from that place. The oracle is what it is, created in a historical context, but like our American Constitution's aim to make of the country a more perfect union, Lenormand must also be viewed with patience and with flexibility. And to stay in this vein for a bit longer, we ought to look at the next card as point/counterpoint to this one.

CARD 29: WOMAN

(Woman, Female Querent or Subject, Feminine, Gentle, Receptive, Yin Energy)

So, again, bearing in mind that Lenormand comes to us from a previous century with different sensibilities in regard to gender identity and sexual orientation, it is important that we learn the card as it was meant to function in this divination system. The Woman (29) may well represent the female-presenting and -identifying seeker sitting across from you. The Woman (29) could also represent someone about whom your seeker is inquiring. Almost as often, though, as is the case with the previous card, the Woman (29) can speak more to the energetic understanding of femaleness—the yin energy to the male yang energy. Therefore, the Woman (29) can represent openness, receptivity, and quietness where the Man (28) is loud, and softness where the Man (28) is hard. The Woman (29) all on its own does not ascribe age or facial features or height specifications to the person it may represent, although such things can be ascertained from the cards that accompany the Woman (29) in a given spread. This fact is the same for the previous Man (28) card. Also, just because the Woman (29) all on its own carries the yin receptive energy vibe, it should not automatically be assumed that the woman in question—if we are indeed talking about an actual woman—is herself possessed of warmth or openness or gentleness. That, too, would be determined by surrounding cards.

• • •

We have one more card to look at in this set of three, and then I will show you some contexts in which the Man (28) and Woman (29) might act out their various roles in particular spreads.

Before we get to that next card, though, I do want to note the fact that some readers believe that Man (28) or Woman (29) should have the word *significator* in the list of keywords given for those cards. I have not done so, because, in my way of reading Lenormand and as I have discussed earlier, *any* Lenormand card can function as significator. In fact, when your sitter has given you a specific area of concern that they would like you to explore, it feels redundant to me to use the Man (28) or Woman (29) card as the significator for your sitter. They are right in front of you. It is a given that they are the one with the question. Instead, I would choose a card representing *the issue* as significator for the spread, ensuring that any information received through that spread would pertain wholly and completely to the issue about which your sitter has concern. More about this later. Now, on to our third card of this latest little trio.

Lily

30

CARD 30: LILY

(Peace, Maturity, Retirement, Ease, Father, Old Age, Sex)

I have always loved the Lenormand Lily (30), for several reasons. First, I call it one of my three "happiness cards" in the deck. The first happiness card I identify as Clover (2), which is quick, unexpected, exciting, ephemeral fun. The second happiness card for me is Bouquet (9), which is the card for beauty, appreciation, all things creative and artistic, from and for which we receive and give admiration and joy. The Lily (30) presents us with a different type of happiness entirely, although it is just as wonderful as the happiness illustrated by her two sisters.

If Clover (2) is the card for a child's excitement upon opening holiday gifts and Bouquet (9) the gifts themselves, then Lily (30) is the card of the satisfied parent, happy in the knowledge that they have provided their child with cause for such exuberant delight, even (especially) if that parent had to work extra hours or make some other sacrifice to give their child a Clover (2)-filled morning. Lily (30) is the card of deep satisfaction and contentment. For example, as I contemplated my retirement after a thirty-year teaching career, the Lily (30) is the card I chose as my significator, my focus card, as I contemplated all the ways I might now fill my extra time, immersing myself in the things I loved solely for the love of them. For example, writing this book that I hope will initiate you into the mysteries of Lenormand could be described in a three-card spread as Book (26) / Lily (30) / Bouquet (9).

There are other meanings ascribed to the Lily (30) beyond simple, contented, peaceful joy. One is that the Lily (30) is the card for the archetypal Father, just as Bear (15) is the card for Mother. Additionally, Lily (30) is the card for an old man—although there is no counterpart for an old woman—whose relative age would need to be ascertained by an examination of the surrounding cards in a given spread. But yes, an old man gets his own card: the Lily (30). When the card takes on that meaning, one should not assume that this father or this old man is necessarily or automatically imbued with the peace, serenity, and calm that are the other meanings of Lily (30). Sometimes, a lily is just a lily, and an old man is just an old man, or a father is just a father. Characteristics, as always, are ascribed to the Lily (30), when it is father or old man, by the surrounding cards.

On a sobering note, I will state unequivocally that whenever I see Lily (30) accompanied closely by Coffin (8), either a literal or figurative demise is imminent. I know how shocking it may feel to see that I have described this as being unerringly true, but in my years of experience, that is exactly what this card combination means. Lilies are, after all, traditional funereal flowers, . . . so there you go. And wouldn't you know that as I type this, what is starting to play on my iPhone but Chopin's Marche Funèbre Piano Sonata No. 2 in B-flat minor, Op. 35—we all know that funeral type of music. A little weird, I grant you. I also assure you, there are no coincidences. Spirit knows I am writing about a card combination that would be naturally accompanied by a piece like this. We are always held, and never alone. Lenormand assures me of that constantly.

On an altogether giddier note, I will add one more meaning for the Lily (30), which will seem to you perhaps almost wildly out of place, given the other meanings for this card. Lily (30) is the traditional

Lenormand card for sex. Surprised? There are actually two cards for sex in the traditional Lenormand deck, the other one being Whip (11). I will leave it to you to decide which card you might choose to use as your significator representing sex in any reading you do. We might be tempted to imagine that each of these two cards speaks to the . . . um . . . degree of enthusiasm or kinkiness involved, but I don't think there is any such traditional association. Nevertheless, you are free to ascribe such meaning to your cards. In other words, tradition-ally speaking, there is no need to assume that the Lily (30) is referring to sedate, once-a-month-only-sex—because-we've-been-married-a-hundred-years. Just as there is no need to assume that the Whip (11) refers to jackrabbit-can't-stop-won't-stop sex. But you could ascribe such meanings to those cards if you wished. Bear in mind that, as ever, the sister cards in a spread with either the Whip (11) or the Lily (30) will serve to either confirm your attribution or dispel it, and it is always better to let your interpretation be guided by the sister cards in such a . . . personal reading, than by the Whip (11) or the Lily (30) alone.

• • •

The practice for the three cards Man (28), Woman (29), and Lily (30) will be pretty quick and obvious. These cards will become far more interesting in the context of larger spreads. For now, though, let's con-sider some quick options.

1. Man (28) / Woman (29) / Lily (30) = The couple (Man 28 / Woman 29) are sexually active (Lily 30) together.

    OR: They are sexually attracted to each other.
    OR: They find peace and contentment together
    (irrespective of sex).

2. Woman (29) / Lily (30) / Man (28) = The woman (Woman 29) prefers (Lily 30) older men (Man 28).

OR:

_____

_____

_____

3. Lily (30) / Man (28) / Woman (29) = The retired (Lily 30) man (Man 28) now has more time to spend with his wife (Woman 29).

OR:

_____

_____

_____

CHAPTER 15

Sun (31) / Moon (32) / Key (33)

Sun

31

CARD 31: SUN

(Warmth, Light, Heat, Summer, Joy, Clarity, Awareness, Revelation, Burn, Fever)

As is the case for most decks in any system, the Lenormand Sun (31) is considered the most positive card of all. The reasons for this are clear, of course. The Sun (31) is our life force. Life without sunlight, at least for Earth, is unsustainable. It is our source of light, helping us to order our days and bring regularity to our lives. We rejoice when the days become longer, because it means we have the opportunity to experience more light as well as more warmth. We attempt to simulate the light and warmth of the Sun (31) during the colder, darker times by using fire and its artificial derivatives, which serve well but are no substitute for the real thing. The Sun (31) is still that to which we turn up our faces in winter so that we may bask in even its weakened rays. More than being life-sustaining, the Sun (31) is life-enhancing. We each have had the experience of waking from sleep and having our mood immediately determined by whether, when we glance out our windows, we witness sky that is sunny and bright or cloudy and gray. We are hardwired to prefer the former to the latter. This point, I think, need not be belabored. We all understand the positive aspects and attributes of that bright orb around which we revolve, both individually during each of our lifetimes and collectively as a planet. There are, however, other aspects to the sun itself, and therefore to the Lenormand Sun (31) card, that are equally worthy of contemplation.

When it comes to timing, the Sun (31) is understandably the card for summer. Clover (2) / Garden (20) / Sun (31), for example, are a lovely combination for outside activities with others during the summer months. It is also true, however, that although we are prone to see the Sun (31) as benign, the principle that there can be too much of a good thing is as operative in relation to the Sun (31) as it is to absolutely everything else. We shield our eyes with sunglasses, and we know not to stare directly into the Sun (31) because our eyes would be damaged as a result. We wear sunscreen and limit our time under the sun's rays, lest our skin burn, age prematurely, or develop a deadly cancer from too much exposure. The Sun (31) is warmth and light, but it is its own entity, burning at its own rate, without regard to result. The Sun (31) is the card for fever, which is, of course, the body's attempt at a healing response to illness. Nevertheless, too high a fever is unsustainable, and so we take fever-reducing medicine and seek out shade and ice to mitigate its effects. Therefore, in any reading where the Sun (31) card appears, it is critical that we remember that the Sun (31) is worthy of both our love, for the life it helps sustain, and also our respect, which the Sun (31) always demands as its due. Global warming, despite what some might say, is the sun's response to being disrespected.

The Sun (31), because it is light as much as it is heat, can act like a searchlight, ferreting out that which would perhaps prefer to remain hidden. Consider this spread:

Fox (14) / Clouds (6) / Snake (7) / Book (26) / Sun (31)

An obfuscating (Clouds 6) professor (Fox 14) may have a nefarious (Snake 7) intention, which they prefer to keep hidden (Book 26), but the truth (Sun 31) will inevitably bring this secret to light.

Conversely, cards such as Fox (14) and Sun (31), when appearing with entirely other cards, can change the story:

Fox (14) / Tree (5) / Book (26) / Letter (27) / Sun (31)

This could well be interpreted to mean:

A doctor (Fox 14) dealing with a thorny medical issue (Tree 5 / Book 26) arrives at a diagnosis (Letter 27) that results in a healing (Sun 31) of the problem.

You see that, in each example, the Sun (31) just does what the Sun (31) does: it shines. The thing upon which the Sun (31) shines, and whether that shining will be for good or for ill, is determined by the Lenormand sister cards that appear with it in a given spread. So, when the Sun (31) appears in any reading, allow yourself that hit of happiness you are bound to feel; then temper that response with one imbued with respect and awe. That way, you allow that golden orb to show you in what way it has chosen to function at that moment, in that spread, which may or may not be what you or your sitter want to see, but will indeed be what is honest and true.

CARD 32: MOON

Moon

32

(*Night, Month, Career, Reputation, Identity, Life Purpose*)

As I have mentioned previously, answers to questions on timing are notoriously nebulous, regardless of what divining system a card reader is using. Again, my theory as to why this is the case has to do with the fact that the diviner is amassing information stored in "the fullness of time," or *kairos* as the Greeks say, and then translating that information into the sort of three-dimensional concept of time according to which human beings order their lives, which the Greeks call *chronos*. I am repeating this mini-lesson on time because, as it happens, the Moon (32) is one of the cards that makes such translation accurate, to the degree possible. As you must surely already know, the Moon (32) is the measure of a month, more or less. The ocean tides and the bodies of women fluctuate according to the movement of the Moon (32). Also, the Moon (32) is most visible at night, so it, along with the Stars (16), would indicate something occurring in the evening, as opposed to during the day. This makes the Moon (32) a useful timing card, though you would be well served to decide in advance of a reading that you intend for the Moon (32) card to serve such a purpose. Therefore, if you are asked a question that specifically has to do with timing, let the Moon (32) speak to you wearing its costume for timing alone.

The Moon (32) has other meanings aside from month and evening, and in a question on timing, you want to set the intention that, should the Moon (32) pop up in your card pull, you do not confuse it for something else. For the purposes of that particular reading, the

Moon (32) is representative of timing alone. On, now, to the other adornments the Moon (32) may come garbed in, when not dressed for a party on timing.

The Moon (32) is the career card. You may recall that when we learned the meanings for Fox (14), one of its most common meanings is job. And I want to make very clear that although sometimes one's job and one's career are the same thing, this is not always the case. Sometimes, one is a kind of subset of the other, and sometimes one has absolutely nothing to do with the other. Therefore, when a sitter comes to me with a question to do with work, I always make sure to have them clarify for me whether they are asking me to look into job or career. This may feel like a bit of hairsplitting to you, but if one is to get a precise and accurate answer to a question, one ought to be sure that the cards are being asked the kind of question that will lend itself to such an answer.

A job is the thing one does to earn one's daily bread. That can be bagging groceries, teaching school, or diagnosing patients. A career can also be bagging groceries, teaching school, or diagnosing patients. What differentiates the job from the career is the desire and the passion with which one engages in any of these activities. If a sitter asks me what their chances of getting this or that job might be, then the Fox (14) would be the focus card, or significator, that I would choose. If a sitter were to ask me about a career shift from one field to another, I would use the Moon (32). The Moon (32) is larger than the Fox (14), when we are thinking about career relative to job. The Moon (32) is the card for the work you feel called to do, rather than the work (Fox 14) you may have fallen into by accident, by default, or to earn extra cash to fund the education you need for your career (Moon 32). See the difference? Again, qualitatively there may be no distinction between Fox (14) and Moon (32), or job and career, but that is not as common as one might both hope and expect. Ideally, one earns a living by doing something one loves. In such a case, the Fox (14) and the

Moon (32) are merged, and sometimes you will see this operative in a reading. More often, though, someone coming for a reading on either work or career may feel a disconnection or a dissonance between the two and is coming to you to receive clarity around this.

More often than you might think, a sitter will ask the incredibly broad and general question, "What is my life's purpose?" The ego part of me—the part I bribe into my car's back passenger seat with snacks and cartoons—wants to answer without the benefit of cards, saying, "Your purpose is to live that life, to enjoy that life, and to leave some love behind in your wake." But no one is asking my ego for its opinion. Therefore, whenever I am asked about "life purpose," I select the Moon (32) as my focus card or significator. The Moon (32) is the card both of reputation and of self-image and self-awareness. The Moon (32) is the card that helps us identify the plot of metaphorical turf upon which we stand and the place from which we move. It is the card for our understanding (or lack thereof) of our right to take up space and air and time. I actually really love reading on the question of life purpose, even though it is exactly the type of question that might make other diviners roll their eyes in frustration. I love it because it is a question that comes from a person's deepest place, and because there is an even deeper place, the Higher Self, from which the answer to this question can flow, through the cards.

For example, let me ask the cards, right in this moment, what my own life's purpose might be. Here is the seven-card spread I pulled, with the Moon (32) as my focus card or significator:

Ring (25) / Whip (11) / Child (13) / Moon (32) / Letter (27) / Sun (31) / Key (33)

We have learned all but one of these cards, so as I read this line, you will get a preview of that Key (33). The sentence I receive from this spread is that my current life's purpose in this moment is to be committed (Ring 25) to writing (Whip 11) a new and simple (Child

13) understanding of Lenormand (Letter 27) so that its mysteries can be illuminated (Sun 31) and unlocked (Key 33). The Moon (32) is in the middle, as it is the focus of the reading in this seven-card spread.

CARD 33: KEY

Key

33

(Answer, Discovery, Enlightenment, Locking or Unlocking)

I call this card the fraternal twin of the Sun (31) card, because it has the potential to be that good, that life-affirming, that illuminating. The presence of the Key (33) in any spread tends to alert us to the fact that whatever answer we seek is just on the horizon. The Key (33) points the way to how and where to go from wherever it is we find ourselves to wherever it is we want to be. The Key (33) reminds us that sometimes it is necessary to both close and lock certain doors to certain rooms in our lives in order that other doors to other rooms may be unlocked, opened, and entered.

The Key (33) is the card of pure potential, both the potential we exercise and the potential that remains just an idea. The Key (33) is the reminder that every single thing our eye beholds began first as a thought. The Key (33) is our map from thought to thing. The Key (33) says to us, "If this . . . then that." The Key (33) is compass, atlas, GPS device. In a Line of Five or Seven, whichever cards follow the Key (33) will indicate next right steps or assured outcomes.

For example, let's go back to our imaginary sitter's question as to whether or not they would receive the job they just applied for. I have pulled cards randomly, with no focus card or significator. It is so much fun to pull this way, because it is kind of like putting a car on automatic pilot and letting Spirit take the wheel.

Key (33) / Letter (27) / Stars (16) / Bear (15) / Fox (14) / Ring (25) / Bouquet (9)

The line advises that the next right action (Key 33) would be to write a note (Letter 27) via email (Stars 16) to whoever it was who interviewed you (Bear 15) thanking them and reiterating your interest in the job (Fox 14). The result of going this extra mile would insure you would be rewarded with a job contract (Ring 25 / Bouquet 9).

Conversely, on that same question, you might pull these cards. The message will sound reminiscent of a previous pull we did, but this time, we have added extra cards we have learned, which serve to flesh out the same, original message.

Fox (14) / Scythe (10) / House (4) / Dog (18) / Bouquet (9) / Key (33) / Crossroads (22)

These cards could indicate that this job your sitter applied for (Fox 14) has already been decided upon (Scythe 10). It will go to someone in-house (House 4) as a reward (Bouquet 9) for their loyalty to the company (Dog 18), and your best course of action (Key 33) would be to set your sights elsewhere and look at other jobs (Cross-roads 22). While this is certainly not news any sitter would want to hear, it is also certainly helpful information: they are now prepared for the disappointment of not getting the job and also given the green light to dust themselves off and look for pastures that may well be far greener. As my mother would say, "Forewarned is forearmed."

• • •

Now let's take a look at our latest three cards and how they might look together in a reading.

1. Sun (31) / Moon (32) / Key (33) = A day (Sun 31) and a night (Moon 32) will pass before the answer (Key 33) will be revealed.

    OR:

    _____

    _____

    _____

2. Moon (32) / Key (33) / Sun (31) = Doing an honest inventory of oneself (Moon 32) is the way (Key 33) to enlightenment (Sun 31).

    OR:

    _____

    _____

    _____

3. Key (33) / Sun (31) / Moon (32) =

    _____

    _____

    _____

    OR:

    _____

    _____

    _____

CHAPTER 16

Fish (34) / Anchor (35) / Cross (36)

Fish

34

CARD 34: FISH

(Emotion, Money, Salary, Flow, Abundance, Many, Much)

Right off, be aware that the Lenormand Fish (34), interpreted broadly, represent two aspects of our lives that are sometimes wildly unrelated and at other times could not be more intimately connected: money and emotion. Of course, we do not necessarily like the idea that these things are as frequently interconnected in our psyches and experience as they are, but the fact of the matter is that the poet Shelley and the physicists have yet to be proven wrong, in that they hypothesize that everything everywhere is not just connected but, ultimately, all the same thing. In the case of the Lenormand Fish (34), this fact is borne out in readings over and over again.

In order to understand how emotion and money might be so intimately connected in the way that Shelley and the physicists mean, I need only remind you of the natural law that assures us that everything is energy. There is nothing that is not energy. What separates one thing from another has literally to do with vibration and then with perception. So how do we understand this link between money and emotion in our lives? How do we separate the one from the other? How do we, as diviners, look at a Lenormand line where the Fish (34) appear and know when we are being shown something solely about emotion, when we are being directed to focus on finance, when we are talking about the interplay between the two, and when the Lenormand Fish (34) are sending us another message entirely? That is where practice and a discerning, attentive third eye and ear are invaluable.

Here are some examples of how Fish (34) might manifest in a variety of ways. First, let's look at a simple three-card spread.

Clover (2) / Fish (34) / Bouquet (9)

These cards, in the absence of a specific question, give a sense that these Fish (34) are a quick run of good fortune, which comes at the exact right time. That run of luck could well have to do with finances. Just as likely, though, is the possibility that these Fish (34) have nothing to do with money. Instead, this trio could speak to a cheerful frame of mind that feels, in and of itself, like a gift. If your sitter had asked you a question about money, you would want to lean toward the first interpretation. If they asked about someone's mood, of course, you would lean toward the second interpretation.

Let's assume that the sitter's question is a financial one, and that they have come into some money and want to know what to do with it. Let's say you decide to pull four more cards at the end of the line, to make it a Line of Seven. What if that line were to read:

Clover (2) / Fish (34) / Bouquet (9) / Crossroads (22) /
Scythe (10) / Clouds (6) / Snake (7)

This might be interpreted to read that the sitter had a choice (Crossroads 22) about what to do with a cache of "found money" (Clover 2 / Fish 34), as in a lottery win for example, with Clover (2) being the card for the sudden and unexpected. Let's say that because this money (Fish 34) feels like a fortuitous gift (Bouquet 9), our sitter has the choice to put the money toward a car payment or to gamble it. Unclear thinking (Clouds 6) would be understandable here, because a sudden windfall could well have that effect on a person's decision-making skills. Therefore, our sitter might be tempted to gamble the money. The Snake (7) at the end of the line implies that this would not be a good use of these "pennies from heaven," and the reading would be caveat against doing something frivolous and irresponsible.

What if our sitter were to come to us with a heavy heart and no question? We might again allow the Fish (34) to serve as our focus card or significator, as we do a reading to locate the nature of the sitter's woes and a possible solution for them. We know in advance, because of our sitter's question, that Fish (34) will represent emotion rather than money in this reading. We pull a Line of Five, with Fish (34) at the center:

Heart (24) / Scythe (10) / Fish (34) / Mountain (21) / Ship (3)

From this reading it seems that our sitter's angst is the result of romantic heartbreak (Heart 24 / Scythe 10) which is preventing them (Mountain 21) from moving on (Ship 3).

As always, the sister cards in a Lenormand spread help direct the reading in the way that it should go. When it comes to the Fish (34) as representative of emotion, it is important to be aware that the term *emotion* can run the gamut from elation to despair, from eagerness to petulance, from superficial to introspective. Again, the sister cards will identify the emotion you and your cards are asked to address. It is unnecessary for you to grill your sitter prior to any reading, and in fact, often the less you know in advance of a reading, the better the reading will be, as it will be uncolored by any preconceptions you may have formed in conversation with your sitter. When I read, all I ask is whether my sitter has an area they would like me to explore. Sometimes, a sitter will want to share details about the issue, but rest assured that in the hands of a skilled diviner, no such preliminary conversation is necessary. Let the cards lead, as they will direct any conversation in ways that will be healing and helpful to your sitter.

When the Lenormand Fish (34) refer to neither money nor emotion, sometimes they can play a considerably more literal role in a reading. For example, they can refer to the sport of fishing itself; they can refer to fish that your sitter is contemplating cooking for dinner; they can refer to that aphorism about there being "more fish in the sea," which is to say your sitter need not settle for what is in front of them as there is more available to them than they realize. The Lenormand Fish (34) can be a complex card, but as is the case with each of the cards, such complexity falls away once the Fish (34) are aligned with her sister cards in a spread and when the diviner uses a light hand and listens for Spirit with an open heart.

CARD 35: ANCHOR

(Job, Security, Safety, Stagnation, Stasis)

The Lenormand Anchor (35) is a fascinating card because it means both one thing and its opposite. We all intuitively understand this fact about the Anchor (35). For example, if a ship is at sea and a storm is brewing, the Anchor (35) can keep a ship from being blown off course by wind gusts. When a ship is at berth, the Anchor (35) is also lowered in order to keep it in its slip during a turbulent night. We talk about "feeling safe and anchored" when we speak of being grounded and centered. In all such cases, the Anchor (35) is benign, helpful, and good.

What happens, though, when a ship remains too long in a harbor and at anchor? Would it not be the case that rust and cranky cogs would result? The same can be said in every case about the Anchor (35). While there are times we need to feel grounded and still or comfortable and safe, we cannot stay in such a state forever without the resultant metaphorical rust taking over. Here is some physics again: "A body at rest stays at rest." It takes a decision in favor of momentum to move from stasis to action, and the problem with the Anchor (35) can be that stasis can come to feel like the more comfortable state. Stasis can indeed feel pleasant: a sort of floating feeling. That is, until it isn't comfortable at all and we realize we have allowed the Anchor (35)'s stasis to sink us deeper than we had ever meant to dive or fall

Here are some examples of how the Lenormand Anchor (35) might function in context of a question. What if a sitter were to ask about whether or not a house move was imminent for them, and you drew the cards:

House (4) / Anchor (35) / Ship (3)

I would be inclined to think that the move would indeed be imminent, because the Anchor (35) here feels as though all is in place for a move to happen. However, if the cards drawn were:

House (4) / Ship (3) / Anchor (35)

I would be inclined to think there would be some holdup or other preventing the move from happening soon, or even at all. The Anchor (35) feels as though it is sinking the move (Ship 3) and holding it back.

What if we were to take that first Line of Three and add cards to it to make the read a five-card spread:

House (4) / Anchor (35) / Ship (3) / Rider (1) / Ring (25) / Letter (27) / Bouquet (9)

These extra cards would confirm my positive feeling about the move being imminent, as the sentence would now read:

The house (House 4) move (Ship 3) is a solid go (Anchor 35) because news is imminent (Rider 1) announcing that the contract for the mortgage (Ring 25 / Letter 27) has been approved (Bouquet 9).

Now let's take that second line, where I interpret the cards to mean that the move will not take place anytime soon, if at all. If we were to pull this longer spread, my intuition would have been confirmed:

House (4) / Ship (3) / Anchor (35) / Mountain (21) / Letter (27) / Ring (25) / Scythe (10)

The house move is held up (House 4 / Ship 3 / Anchor 35) because a delay (Mountain 21) in the paperwork (Letter 27) means the deal (Ring 25) falls through (Scythe 10).

The Lenormand Anchor (35) can portend help or hindrance. The sister cards decide which role any given Anchor (35) will play in any given spread. I should also add that the Anchor (35) is one of the two Lenormand cards that can stand for a job, the other card being Fox (14). I would advise that early in your reading career, you select one of the two cards as your work/job card. Mine is the Fox (14), but the Anchor (35) is also traditional, so feel free to use it instead of the Fox (14).

Cross

36

CARD 36: CROSS

(Any Religion, Burden, Ending, Pain,
Sorrow, Pro Bono Work, Sacrifice,
Altruism)

For reasons which should be obvious,
and as tends to be the case when the
Coffin (8) appears in a reading, diviners and sitters alike can experience the
kind of wariness that creates a catch
in the throat and a widening of the
eyes whenever the Cross (36) shows
up. Like the Coffin (8), the Lenormand Cross (36) can conjure images
of potential pain and emotional endings. And, as is true for the Coffin
(8) when its meaning is transformation, there are ways in which the
Cross (36) also acts as a harbinger of hope. But let's walk through this
card's fire before we quench that fire at hope's river.

The Cross (36), as we all know, is the symbol for Christianity. Of
course, before it became the symbol for a preeminent world religion,
it was a crucifix, an instrument of torture and execution invented by
the Persians and made infamous by the Romans. It literally means the
affixing of someone to a T-bar, and this was generally done by ham-
mering nails into the hands and feet of the doomed. Death came, if
not from the shock and pain, from asphyxia, as it would have become
harder and harder for the shoulders to support the weight of the body,
making it difficult to breathe. This was not a quick process, by any
means. The Lenormand Cross (36) mimics this sense of prolonged
pain when the card takes on this difficult aspect. The experience
of pain is an inescapable part of being human, of course. Its nature,
source, depth, and duration are variable and relative—and sometimes
self-inflicted. All such details can be discerned when the Cross (36)

is considered in conjunction with her Lenormand sisters. Sometimes, the Cross (36) signifies an unequivocal ending to a situation, as can the Coffin (8). Unlike the Coffin (8), however, where an ending can herald a new beginning, the Lenormand Cross (36), when it appears as an ending, offers no such mitigation. Cross (36) endings are painful—period. There are times, however, when the Cross (36) is something other, and perhaps more, than pain and endings.

The Cross (36) is the card, for example, of sacrifice and altruism, volunteerism and pro bono work. This is because these are things which, while we may offer them willingly, cost us something in regard to time and effort we could be otherwise expending or conserving for our own personal ends. I hope you have had the experience of offering someone something they needed with no expectation of recompense for your generosity. If so, then you understand this meaning of the Lenormand Cross (36): sometimes, even though you have lost something, having given it away (time, money, effort), you have, in fact, been enriched in the giving. Say, for example, you are really hungry, have no food in the house, and order a pizza. You are looking forward to eating all of those eight slices by yourself, one after the other. Suppose then, that following hard upon the pizza delivery, eight hungry friends show up at your door. If you were operating from the place of the Lenormand Cross (36), you would not look for your pizza slicer and divvy the pie up so that every one of you could have a little. You would let your eight friends eat those eight slices, without thought to your own hunger. Of course, that is a silly example, but it is indeed an example. Here is how a version of that story might look if I were to tell it in the language of Lenormand:

Bear (15) / House (4) / Dog (18) / Mice (23) / Bouquet (9) / Coffin (8) / Cross (36)

You arrive home ravenous (Bear 15 / House 4), and some friends show up (Dog 18) who are feeling stressed (Mice 23), so you gift them (Bouquet 9) with food and your time even though all you want to do is eat and go to bed (Coffin 8 / Cross 36). You have made this sacrifice for your friends, and as tired as you are, you feel good about yourself because you did something kind when you were not required to do it. That is the Lenormand Cross (36) in action, albeit on a micro scale. In the macro, the Lenormand Cross (36) can take the form of any act of altruism, from serving in the Peace Corps to adopting a child. Even childbirth itself, where one's body acts as host to a guest who grows and takes for nine months and then leaves in no gentle manner, can, with correct accompanying cards, be symbolized by the Cross (36):

Child (13) / Stork (17) / Whip (11) / Bear (15) / Cross (36)

• • •

The Cross (36), a card of endings, also brings us to the end of our walk through the Lenormand's thirty-six traditional cards. We will look at how our last three cards might function together in short spreads, and then we will explore a Nine Box Spread for cards 28–36, before moving on to other spreads beyond the three-, five-, seven-, and nine-card spreads we have been practicing throughout this book.

First, our traditional final three:

1. Fish (34) / Anchor (35) / Cross (36) = She felt emotionally (Fish 34) stuck (Anchor 35) after ending things (Cross 36) with him.

   OR:

   _____

   _____

   _____

2. Anchor (35) / Cross (36) / Fish (34) = He stayed for so long (Anchor 35) at a job (Anchor 35) he didn't like (Cross 36) because he needed the money (Fish 34).

OR:

_____

_____

_____

3. Cross (36) / Fish (34) / Anchor (35) =

_____

_____

_____

OR:

_____

_____

_____

CHAPTER 17

Nine Box for Cards 28–36

N ow let's look at a Nine Box Spread for cards 28–36. As before, I will shuffle these nine cards and then lay the cards out in the order they decide to show themselves. That way, the cards, rather than I as the diviner, will dictate the subject of this reading. While these cards can be pulled from the top or the bottom, I love pulling a Nine Card Spread using the Fibonacci sequence, which I am showing you here for the first time, even though I used it to pull the other Nine Box Spreads we have discussed. The spreads on shown on page 146. The cards are pulled in this order:

Fibonacci Sequence

Card 8	Card 4	Card 9
Card 3	Card 1	Card 5
Card 7	Card 2	Card 6

For our nine-card spread using only cards 28–36, I have drawn:

Fish (34)	Woman (29)	Cross (36)
Anchor (35)	Moon (32)	Key (33)
Man (28)	Sun (31)	Lily (30)

1. The center card this time is Moon (32). This will be the subject of our reading. We have not posed any question, but the Moon (32) tells us that the subject of the reading will be career.

2. The next thing to look at would be the corner cards of the spread. They help us to further identify the spread's theme, which we already suspect has something to do with retirement based on the presence of Moon (32) and Lily (30). These cards are read clockwise, from the top left corner:

Fish (34) / Cross (36) / Lily (30) / Man (28)

3. Since we know we are talking about retirement, perhaps the sitter is worried about how their financial situation will be once they are no longer employed.

4. The vertical cards give us a sense of the past, present, and future of this person, in regard to career matters. The first vertical—Fish (34) / Anchor (35) / Man (28)—suggests that this sitter has been at this job for some considerable time and may have some emotions they have needed to sort out in regard to this longevity. Fish (34) stand for emotions here, and the Anchor (35) is an alternate job card. The Anchor (35) also implies longevity, remaining in one place for an extended period of time. The second vertical line speaks of the situation as it is now—Woman (29) / Moon (32) / Sun (31). Our sitter may want to rethink career at this point, and perhaps spend some time relaxing on a sunny vacation with the one he loves. Our third vertical line will give us a sense of what is to come—Cross (36) / Key (33) / Lily (30). It would seem that, as painful as the prospect may be, this is the right time to consider retirement.

5. The next thing to look at are the horizontal lines. The top horizontal line identifies the sitter's thoughts about this matter—Fish (34) / Woman (29) / Cross (36). The sitter's partner is particularly concerned about postretirement cash flow. The center horizontal line, which moves thought into action, is Anchor (35) / Moon (32) / Key (33), suggesting that the answer to this problem could be some sort of postretirement employment. The bottom horizontal line addresses the situation's undercurrent, and things of which the sitter may be as yet unaware—Man (28) / Sun (31) / Lily (30). The sitter will really love being retired. Even if they do move on to some other position, they are ready to leave where they are for pastures they have reason to believe will be greener than the one in which they have spent so many long years.

6. The diagonal lines are the next ones to consider. They portend movement and flow, and are read from the top left to the bottom right and then from the bottom left to the top right. These lines

of flow are Fish (34) / Moon (32) / Lily (30) and then Man (28) / Moon (32) / Cross (36). It seems money will not be an issue and is something they can relax about. Also, retirement will be an opportunity for this couple to become reacquainted with each other in a way that life may have made hard; a sort of second honeymoon, where they can meet as two new people they just found.

7. Finally, we can mirror all but the center card (Moon 32), and this should give us some confirmatory information.

- Fish (34) mirrors Man (28) = This is an emotional decision for our sitter.

- Fish (34) mirrors Cross (36) = Money flow in retirement has been a concern, and perhaps is what even has delayed the retirement to date.

- Fish (34) mirrors Lily (30) = Retirement is emotional *and* requires money managing.

- Woman (29) mirrors Sun (31) = The sitter's partner looks forward to a vacation somewhere warm to kick off this retirement.

- Cross (36) mirrors Lily (30) = However much our sitter looks forward to retirement, it is always hard to say goodbye. Cross (36) mirroring Man (28) confirms this.

- Anchor (35) mirrors Key (33) = A postretirement job will be a terrific idea for our sitter.

- Man (28) mirrors Lily (30) = Our sitter is ready to retire. *But* Cross (36) mirroring Man (28) is more confirmation that this is not an easy decision.

As you see, this Nine Box Spread has provided a plethora of information for your sitter. Remember that with this spread, as is also true for the Lines of Three, Five, and Seven, you need not choose the Man (28) or Woman (29) card to represent your sitter, as the fact that you are reading for them is implicit. A far more effective and efficient use of the cards is to get right to the heart of the matter and use your spread's central card to represent the issue about which your sitter has concerns. And a wonderful way to watch Spirit at work from beginning to end of any spread is also to simply let the cards decide what will be the central card—the card that represents what is uppermost in your sitter's mind, whether they are conscious of it or not. Invariably, that center card will focus and direct the reading exactly where it needs to go, and your sitter will be relieved and perhaps changed in all the best ways by realizing they are always held, always guided, and never alone and that the Universe knows what is on their heart and how best to heal it. All of this awareness can be realized and recognized when the cards are read by a skilled and compassionate diviner whose single purpose is to help the sitter in this way.

CHAPTER 18

The Grand Tableau

Now that we have practiced all of the smaller traditional spreads, it is time to advance to the spread that can first awe and intimidate and then enlighten and inform in tremendous ways, and that is the Lenormand Grand Tableau. This spread incorporates all thirty-six traditional cards. We have studied each of these cards individually. We understand that they are archetypal in nature, making each card identifiable and autonomous. That said, it is important to remember that reading Lenormand is, above all, a "group activity." No single Lenormand card can move from static to fluid without consideration of and consultation with her sister cards. Each card's sisters serve to explicate, elaborate, enhance, and elucidate by turning word into sentence, and then sentences into story. Whether comprised of three, five, seven, or nine cards, each story the sisters tell is rich with meaning, and the Lenormand Grand Tableau is the equivalent of a multivolume epic saga. That is the reason it can feel so intimidating.

The secret to move from intimidation to understanding is to keep in mind that the Grand Tableau is actually a compilation of all the line and box techniques we have already covered. A good analogy might be to think of the experience of having a subject pique your interest, whereupon you go to the library and discover a huge and heavy tome on that subject, which promises to answer your every question. The size and weight of that tome might be such that you need a cart to carry it to your study table. Once settled at your table, however, you would approach learning its contents the way you would the contents of any book: one page at a time. The Lenormand Grand Tableau ought to be approached in the same way: line by line and box by box. There are a couple of traditional ways of reading this enormous spread. Mine is perhaps best described as a hybrid approach, which I hope you will enjoy.

What follows are a couple of charts to show you the spread layout. I will say a couple of things about these charts, and then I will order the steps I take when approaching the Grand Tableau. That way, you will have a sample one to use for reference and a set of instructions and a template to turn to when you draw a Grand Tableau for yourself or your sitter.

The Grand Tableau Spread Layout

1	2	3	4	5	6	7	8
9	10	11	12	13	14	15	16
17	18	19	20	21	22	23	24
25	26	27	28	29	30	31	32
		33	34	35	36		

As you see, I have written out the card numbers 1–36. Here is the same information, but using card names instead. I highly encourage you to memorize both each card and its meanings *and* its number. In Romance languages such as French, for example, one does not ever learn a vocabulary word without also learning its article (*La chat* = the cat / *Le chien* = the dog). Every noun in French has a masculine or feminine *the* in the form of *le* or *la*. As with French, so with the French oracle Lenormand, which is to say every card's number is as important as the picture the card portrays, as these numbers will help you read the Grand Tableau with elegance and facility. So here are the same thirty-six cards in the Grand Tableau layout, but with their words. You should practice saying them together until you could do any Lenormand reading with the numbers alone:

Rider / Clover / Ship / House / Tree / Clouds / Snake / Coffin

Bouquet / Scythe / Whip / Birds / Child / Fox / Bear / Stars

Stork / Dog / Tower / Garden / Mountain / Crossroads / Mice / Heart

Ring / Book / Letter / Man / Woman / Lily / Sun / Moon

Key / Fish / Anchor / Cross

I am taking such pains with this because we are looking at the Grand Tableau, which presents us with an opportunity to explore not only lines and boxes, but also layers of meaning within lines and boxes. The two charts presented above show you the cards in their native settings. For example, the first card is Rider. The Rider's home is in that first position, just as the Cross's native setting, its home, is in last position, 36. I am calling these settings *native* and *home* because, in fact, these positions are referred to in the Grand Tableau as *Houses*. Houses are what will later allow us to layer meaning, and so I again entreat you to learn both the meanings of the cards as well as each card's number. I promise that such study will, in the end, take your Lenormand reading from good to great. Now, let us return to what we are already well-versed in, which are lines and boxes. We will come back to Houses later on.

The Grand Tableau is a spread comprised of lines and boxes, which will provide you with information about any conceivable topic about which you might inquire. Because the future is not written in stone, the cards are mutable and fluid. A GT drawn for a specific period of predetermined time—a month, three months, a year—can show you what the current trajectory appears to be in all areas of life, as well as a general overview of what kind of year the sitter may anticipate. From this information, of course, decisions and directions can be made and changed and adjusted, so as to affect the outcome within certain parameters.

I would not be inclined to throw a spread as large as the Grand Tableau for a single answer to a single question; there are other, smaller, better spreads for that. But to get a little information on a lot of areas, the Grand Tableau is invaluable.

STEPS FOR READING A GRAND TABLEAU

1. Select a deck you think you would enjoy working with. If it is a modern deck with extra cards beyond the traditional thirty-six, remove those cards from the deck for the purposes of this spread.

2. Select a flat surface upon which to read. Any surface will work—a table, a floor, a bed—so long as that surface provides sufficient space for the laying out of all thirty-six cards.

3. Shuffle your deck using whatever method you find comfortable. Lenormand cards are never read using reversals, which is to say that all cards are always read right side up. Therefore, if you shuffle by spreading the cards on the table and kind of pushing them around until you feel they are sufficiently shuffled, when you gather them up, you may find some of them are upside-down. When you put them on your reading surface, they will need to be placed right side up.

4. As you shuffle, decide upon a time frame for the reading. Again, this can be as short as a week and as long as a year. I would not use this spread for anything either shorter or longer than these time frames. For shorter time frames, other spreads are more efficient and accurate, and for longer time frames, Lenormand might serve to preempt and be disrespectful of the nature and power of free will. Lenormand is an oracle grounded in your real lived context, and I think it important to let the energy of a situation play out a bit, rather than trying to read too far out into the future, which might limit your options too severely.

5. After shuffling, it is time to lay out the cards in the order I outlined above: pulling from the top of the deck, you will lay your cards in four lines of eight cards each. This will leave you with four cards still in your hand, which you will center below your final line of eight.

SAMPLE READING

On page 156 I have presented a sample Grand Tableau for an imaginary female sitter. Once we have read for her, you will be fully able to read for yourself, and then, with practice, for actual sitters. The card images are shown on page 157.

Here are the cards:

Stars (16) / Letter (27) / Key (33) / Ship (3) / Coffin (8) / Birds (12) / Dog (18) / Mice (23)

Woman (29) / Anchor (35) / Clover (2) / Snake (7) / Bear (15) / Mountain (21) / Book (26) / Moon (32)

House (4) / Bouquet (9) / Child (13) / Tower (19) / Heart (24) / Man (28) / Fish (34) / Rider (1)

Scythe (10) / Fox (14) / Garden (20) / Ring (25) / Sun (31) / Tree (5) / Whip (11) / Stork (17)

Crossroads (22) / Lily (30) / Cross (36) / Clouds (6)

And, for practice without the words, here is the chart with just the numbers:

16	27	33	3	8	12	18	23
29	35	2	7	15	21	26	32
4	9	13	19	24	28	34	1
10	14	20	25	31	5	11	17
	22	30	36	6			

Mice 23

 Moon 32

 Rider 1

 Stork 17

 Dog 18

 Book 26

 Fish 34

 Whip 11

 Birds 12

 Mountain 21

 Man 28

 Tree 5

 Clouds 6

 Coffin 8

 Bear 15

 Heart 24

 Sun 31

 Cross 36

 Ship 3

 Snake 7

 Tower 19

 Ring 25

 Lily 30

 Key 33

 Clover 2

 Child 13

 Garden 20

 Crossroads 22

 Letter 27

 Anchor 35

 Bouquet 9

 Fox 14

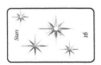 Stars 16

 Woman 29

 House 4

 Scythe 10

ORDER OF OPERATIONS PART I

1. I am going to assume that my sitter is a woman, and that she has asked me to look at her year ahead. Therefore, I will look for where the Woman (29) is in the spread. If she is relatively high up, as she is here, the indication is that she will be in control and aware of much that will happen during the course of the next year. If she had been lower down in the spread, she would have had less agency and aegis, and there would be considerably more surprises waiting in the wings. If Woman (29) had appeared as one of the final four cards in the spread, she would be anticipated to spend the year more acted upon than actor, more observer than performer. But here, she is considered to be fairly high up in the spread, so there are no worries on that count. She is in a good position.

2. Next, I look at the four corners of the spread, which in our case study are cards 16, 23, 17, and 10, and I read them clockwise, beginning with the top left card and ending with the bottom left card. These cards provide information as to the sitter's theme for the year. Given what you have learned about Lines of Three and Five, what would you say this line of four might say about our sitter's overarching theme for the year?

    Stars (16) / Mice (23) / Stork (17) / Scythe (10) look to me as though our sitter is excited about the upcoming year and is going to make some decisions to make improvements from last year. Does that make sense? How else might you read this line?

    _____

    _____

    _____

    _____

3. For still more information as to the year's theme, I look now to the first four cards of the spread: 16 / 27 / 33 / 3. What might we say about Stars (16) / Letter (27) / Key (33) / Ship (3)? Perhaps our sitter will be in virtual correspondence about a move that will prove pivotal. How else might you interpret this line?

    _____

    _____

    _____

    _____

4. Finally, to get to the heart of the matter, I would look to the cards referred to as the heart of the spread. These cards are in original House positions 12, 13, 20, and 21. Meaning, if we were to count from 1 to 36, we would look to see which cards have landed in these spots this time, spots that are the home base of Birds (12), Child (13) / Garden (20), and Mountain (21). In our practice spread for our imaginary woman sitter, however, the cards that appear in these positions, the ones that make up the heart of the spread, are in fact cards 7, 15, 19, 24. These are Snake (7) / Bear (15) / Tower (19) / Heart (24). What might we say about this line?

    _____

    _____

    _____

    _____

And further, to take a sharper spade and dig a deeper level down, what might it say to us that the Snake (7) is in the House of the Birds (12)? That the Bear (15) is in the House of the Child (13)? That the Tower (19) is in the House of the Garden (20)? That the Heart (24) is in the House of the Mountain (21)? Perhaps there will be unpleasant exchanges with friends or associates? Perhaps our sitter will be spending time with her mother, seeking comfort from her after these exchanges? Perhaps our sitter will feel as though she needs some time away from social interaction in order to heal fully from these rifts with friends or associates. Can you see how I arrived at these conclusions? What other thoughts come to you when looking at these cards that are the heart of the spread and the Houses in which we find them?

_____

_____

_____

_____

Notice that all I am doing is reading short lines, just as I have been teaching you to do all along. Page by page we are exploring this huge tome. We proceed nibble by nibble, rather than gulp by gulp.

5. Speaking of tomes, if you are anything like me, when you read a particularly suspenseful book, you may be tempted to skip ahead to learn whodunit and why. In the Lenormand Grand Tableau, the way to read ahead in the story is to look at those last stand-alone cards, in House positions 33, 34, 35, and 36. In our sample GT for our imaginary sitter, these cards are 22, 30, 36, 6. What might Crossroads (22) / Lily (30) / Cross (36) / Clouds (6) mean? Perhaps that the upcoming year will culminate in our sitter having some decisions to make that will bring her some peace and contentment and end whatever she has found frustrating and confusing. If we take our sharpened spade and dig yet deeper, we learn that the Crossroads (22) is in the House of the Key (33); the Lily (30) is in the House of the Fish (34); the Cross (36) is in the House of the Anchor (35); and the Clouds (6) are in the House of the Cross (36). This tells us that making the choice in favor of emotional peace and ease is a wise one, that her emotional equilibrium will depend on achieving such a state of ease, that she is

totally over feeling painfully stuck, and that she needs to figure out how she got in that state in the first place. What else might these cards mean?

———————————————————————————
———————————————————————————
———————————————————————————
———————————————————————————
———————————————————————————
———————————————————————————

Certainly, we want to keep in mind our initial understanding that our sitter, high up in the spread as she is, will be up to any challenge, will learn to separate the wheat in her life from the chaff, and will come out the better for it. Friend groups may change, but that is the way of things, is it not? Such sorting can make room for better, more authentic, less contentious relationships to be found and nurtured.

RECAP

1. Locate your sitter in the spread.

2. Examine the spread's four corners to assess the theme.

3. Assess the first four cards in the spread for more theme information/confirmation.

4. Go to the heart of the spread in House positions 12, 13, 20, 21. The cards sitting in those Houses will help you take a really granular look at the overall theme.

5. Take a glance at the spread's final four cards, found in House positions 33, 34, 35, 36. They will help you to "read ahead" in the story to see how things will end up.

ORDER OF OPERATIONS PART II

Locate your sitter again: Woman (29) in our current spread. We are next going to practice familiar skills, as we are going to look at lines, which you are well used to reading by now.

1. What are the cards in the vertical line in which Woman (29) appears, and what assessment can you make about them? In our sample reading, the vertical line in which we see Woman (29) is 16, 29, 4, 10, or Stars (16) / Woman (29) / House (4) / Scythe (10). Perhaps the line means that our sitter will decide to cut off her social media and keep herself more to herself. This would certainly be consistent with other assessments we have made so far in this GT.

2. What are the cards in the horizontal line which contains Woman (29)? In this sample reading, Woman (29) appears first. The cards are 29, 35, 2, 7, 15, 21, 26, 32. In words, the line reads Woman (29) / Anchor (35) / Clover (2) / Snake (7) / Bear (15) / Mountain (21) / Book (26) / Moon (32). This is only one card longer than the seven-card readings we have practiced before. What sentence might you make from this line? Perhaps it reads something like this:

Our sitter, originally feeling safe and happy, hits a rough patch that she did not see coming, and it will affect her sense of self. Is this not consistent with what we have already learned, such that we know our sitter will need and want time and space for recovery from some emotional injury caused by some social slight? How else might you interpret this horizontal line?

3. Now it is time to look at the diagonal lines in which Woman (29) appears. If you recall from our study of the Nine Box Spread, the diagonals represent flow and movement. We can tell from these lines whether our sitter's year will go from good to great, from better to worse, from bad to awful, or to some other spectrum iteration. As we read these particular diagonals, our lines are: 29, 9, 20. The bottom four cards of the spread are not to be counted as part of either the vertical or horizontal lines, which is why we have only three cards here. These three together, Woman (29) / Bouquet (9) / Garden (20), indicate a person who loves to be in nature, as well as out and about in public. Being outside in any way feels to her like a gift and a blessing. Our other diagonal in which Woman (29) appears is shorter still, as it is only two cards: Letter (27) / Woman (29). This diagonal is really too short to tell us much of anything, except that perhaps our sitter has paperwork to address or enjoys writing. We can let that line go. We will find more information elsewhere. Remember that the diagonals are about flow. Our sitter is a literate woman who is fond of the outdoors. Perhaps these facts will be ones that sustain her during the course of any trials she may face.

4. Finally, we look to see if Woman (29) can be made the center of a Nine Box Spread, something with which, by now, we are comfortably familiar. In our sample GT, Woman (29) cannot, in fact, be centered in a Nine Box, because she is on the spread's outer edge. She can, however, be part of a Nine Box that will have another card at its center. The cards for this Nine Box are:

Stars (16) / Letter (27) / Key (33)

Woman (29) / Anchor (35) / Clover (2)

House (4) / Bouquet (9) / Child (13)

The Woman (29) is our focus for this GT, but because she is not able to be placed in the center of this Nine Box, our attention should immediately go to whatever card *is* in the center of the Nine Box in which Woman (29) plays any part at all. As we see above, the Anchor (35) is in the center of this Nine Box, and so this woman's security and stability in all areas of her life are critical during the time period covered by this GT. We have already established this to be the case through the reading of other lines of this spread, but in this Nine Box, we go through the same process as we always do when examining any Nine Box Spread, this time with an eye toward our sitter's security and stability. We are expecting to see corroborative evidence of what we have already learned, so let's look at the box systematically to find out if this hypothesis is correct.

Vertical lines indicating past, present, and future:

- Past: Stars (16) / Woman (29) / House (4) = The sitter has had concerns about her domestic situation.

- Present: Letter (27) / Anchor (35) / Bouquet (9) = The sitter either is hoping for or else has indeed received paperwork about her situation which has or will please her.

- Future: Key (33) / Clover (2) / Child (13) = This line confirms that there will be some resolution to her concerns about stability that will make her very happy, and perhaps provide her with a new start and outlook.

Horizontal lines indicating what the sitter's thoughts are, how and to what extent these thoughts will turn into action, and any underlying events and circumstances that will affect the stability situation:

- Top for Thoughts: Stars (16) / Letter (27) / Key (33) = The sitter is hoping for a sort of deus ex machina event, whereby something in writing will be presented to her that will be the answer to her stability concerns. This could be a rental or mortgage agreement, a check that arrives, or really anything in writing that she would see as pivotal to resolution of this issue.

- Center for Thoughts Turned to Action: Woman (29) / Anchor (35) / Clover (2) = It seems that the sitter's thoughts have indeed morphed into things, because the very wish she made in the top horizontal line seems to have come true.

- Bottom for Underlying Factors: House (4) / Bouquet (9) / Child (13) = A new housing situation is what this security issue was all about, and even though our sitter may be downsizing (Child 13), it will be a perfect resolution with Bouquet (9) confirming her satisfaction with this situation.

- Diagonal Lines Indicating Movement and Flow: Stars (16) / Anchor (35) / Child (13) as well as House (4) / Anchor (35) / Key (33) are both lines that speak to positive movement for this sitter in regard to her housing and its role in causing her to feel comfortable and stable. Downsizing seems like a perfect solution to her issue.

• • •

Here is a tip that I hope you will love:

We began our study of this Grand Tableau by locating the female sitter. It is also the case that we need not have started with her, but instead, with any of the thirty-six cards at all. For example, if our sitter had said that she was particularly concerned about her financial situation, we could have begun our reading with the Bear (15) or Fish (34) and looked at the vertical, horizontal, and diagonal lines in which either of those cards appeared. We could also have looked at the Nine Box that held the Bear (15) or Fish (34) at its center or on its periphery. Every piece of information we would have gleaned from such examination would have had exclusively to do with our sitter's financial situation. If the Bear (15) had been the card on which we concentrated, we would have been examining our sitter's overall financial stability. If we had chosen to focus on Fish (34), then cash flow would have been our core concern.

Had our sitter asked us to concentrate on her career, we would have used the Moon (32) as our focus card, and all the steps we did when we used Woman (29), we would have followed with the Moon

(32) as our central point of orientation. For a move, we would have used Ship (3); for the state of her marriage, Ring (25). You get the picture, so to speak, I hope. Any card can be the focus of a Grand Tableau, not just the Man (28) or Woman (29) cards. This fact is what makes the Grand Tableau such an involved spread: you can find out something about everything using such a spread.

To do the spread justice requires much time and patience, which is why it is not a spread I would do often or lightly. Just to make the case for how involved a spread the Grand Tableau is, in the next chapter I will show you two more techniques you can add to your reading of it. Although I prefer one over the other, I do them both, because one is the long form and one is the short form—it's similar to the different ways one can do division problems in math: you will arrive at the same answer no matter which form you use, and therefore, one technique can be a check against the other, if you wish.

CHAPTER 19

Chaining and Counting

Remember my telling you how important it is for you to memorize the thirty-six Lenormand card numbers, because they are as important as the pictures themselves? It may have driven you crazy to see that I have accompanied each card name with its number every single time I referenced it, but it was a calculated move for such a time as this. In addition to your Lenormand deck, you will want some paper and a pen for this next step.

CHAINING

Recall that I told you that each Lenormand card has a home that is native to it. For example, the home native to the Rider (1) is position 1 in the Grand Tableau. The home that is native to the Cross (36) is position 36. You can look back to see where I have laid that out for you on page 152. These homes are referred to as Houses. Even the House (4) has its own home, as it is native to position 4. When the cards are all laid out in numerical order, in four horizontal lines of eight cards each, with the final four cards centered underneath that fourth line, you will have placed each card in its own house.

Of course, when you shuffle your cards and lay them out to do a Grand Tableau, the cards will, statistically speaking, most often land in some other House than the one each is native to. For example, in the Grand Tableau I laid out for you earlier, the Woman (29), which is the card representing our sitter, is found in the House of the Bouquet (position 9). We know that the Bouquet (9) is a reward, a gift, something to do with the visual and performing arts. Therefore, the fact that our sitter (Woman 29) is in this House of Bouquet (9) means that something good is coming her way, in the form of art or beauty or a gift or reward.

To create a chain, we will write down the words *Woman/Bouquet*. Then we will look to see where the Bouquet (9) is located. Since the Woman (29) is in the Bouquet (9)'s home, or House, that Bouquet (9) must be somewhere else. As it happens, we find it in position 18, which is the House of the Dog (18). Now our chain reads *Woman/Bouquet/Dog*.

Next, as Dog (18) has been relocated elsewhere because its House is otherwise occupied by the Bouquet (9), we must see where that Dog (18) has landed. We find it in the House of the Snake (7), so we add that card as the latest in our chain. We continue to look for cards that have been displaced from their own Houses until we return back to our original card, which is Woman (29). For the sake of expediency, I will do the rest of the chain so you can see it all together:

Woman (29) / Bouquet (9) / Dog (18) / Snake (7) / Birds (12) /

Clouds (6) / Cross (36) / Anchor (35) / Scythe (10) / Ring (25) /

Man (28) / Crossroads (22) / Key (33) / Ship (3) / House (4) /

Stork (17) / Moon (32) / Stars (16) / Rider (1) / Heart (24) /

Mountain (21) / Fox (14) / Book (26) / Bear (15) / Child (13) /

Tower (19) / Garden (20) / Letter (27) / Clover (2) / Whip (11) /

Sun (31) / Woman (29)

From this list of cards, you will string together a story that starts out something like this: Our sitter feels blessed in her friendships, but

The Language of Lenormand

there are those in her circle who engage in gossip about her, which she finds painful. This causes her to make some decisions about whom to keep and whom to cut out of her life, and these decisions cause her to be able to move forward in a much happier state.

Do you see how I arrived at that from reading the story of this chain? Again, you can chain from any card in the Grand Tableau, in order to get more granular information about the card at which you start your chain. Sometimes, chains are startlingly short. Sometimes, it feels as though you will never arrive back at your starting point. It took us chaining sixteen cards to get to the end of this story. The next method I will show you takes care of that problem in very short order.

COUNTING

This method is actually a streamlined version of chaining. I will list the steps here and that will become immediately clear.

1. Locate the card representing the issue you want to look at. Here, we will again start with Woman (29) to get an overview of what will be most important for our sitter.

2. Woman (29) will be card #1. We will then count from #1 to #9, and whatever that ninth card is, we will write it down: Woman (29) / House (4). Then, we will count every fourth card, until we return back to Woman (29). Therefore, our counting will look like this, once we are done:

Woman (29) / House (4) / Heart (24) / Scythe (10) / Sun (31) / Crossroads (22) / Stars (16) / Coffin (8) / Woman (29)

Notice that we are taking eight cards to tell a very similar story: Our sitter, feeling happy and at home with life, had her heart broken in a way that caused her to reassess and ultimately make choices that will prove transformative for her moving forward.

Perhaps this counting method will strike you as the CliffsNotes version of what we arrived at by chaining, and I won't disagree. I hope you also see why doing both methods in any Grand Tableau is indeed a good check on your work. Nothing has contradicted anything else we have seen elsewhere in this Grand Tableau, which is the point.

And again, as with chaining, you can begin with any card. If your sitter wants to know about their health, and you are someone who reads on such matters, then begin your chaining and counting from the Tree (5). If they have concerns about their marriage, begin your reading (including chaining and counting) from the Ring (25).

• • •

Taken altogether, a Grand Tableau with all of its lines, boxes, and its counting, chains, and Houses is an impressive, comprehensive spread that deserves respect. Every sitter who comes to your table is not in need of such a spread, particularly when they come to you with specific questions that could be more efficiently and quickly answered by the drawing of Lines of Three, Five, or Seven, and certainly by a Nine Box Spread. I would advise saving the Grand Tableau for those clients who come to you annually and want an overview of their year. As I mentioned, I used to draw a Grand Tableau for myself on a monthly basis. Now, I will draw one around the time of my birthday and at the New Year. In between, the smaller spreads suffice.

I do have a secret up my sleeve, however, which will satisfy those of you who worry that, while a Grand Tableau may be too big a spread to draw every time for every client, a spread as small as three or even nine cards will not do your client justice. Get ready for the bonus section coming up next, in which I will show you the spread I use most often, which I created very early in my reading career for just this reason.

CHAPTER 20

The Twenty-Three–Card Erika's Reading

I have made mention several times of the fact that, for me, reading Lenormand is never anything less than an exercise in spiritual healing, both of myself and of those who seek me out. Not everyone chooses to see Lenormand in this way, and I respect their autonomy. I just know that when I learned to set aside ego and looked for a different partner in my reading, Spirit, Higher Self, the Universe, God—and I use all of these terms interchangeably—was what stepped into the breach where my ego had previously been.

To make my case, I will tell you the story of how I arrived at the spread I am about to teach you next. I will leave it to you to decide whether the story is all just my imagination. And if that turns out to be your conclusion, I would ask you, why would that be a problem? The mind is a world unto itself. Whether you consider yourself a spiritually oriented person or not, if you allow your mind to expand, your reading will soar. Here's my story:

Early in my Lenormand learning, back in the days when there were only a couple of online communities and most resources were in French and German only, I set about teaching myself the system. I was a new widow back then, a parent with a teenager to raise, a high school teacher at the beginning of a new academic year, surrounded by people full of sympathetic looks and few words to say. Widows, I think, must be difficult to be around, reminders as we are of the frailty of human existence and of the unexpectedness that awaits each of us around every corner. Determined not to burden those around me with my bewilderment and my grief, I found the cards to be for me the kind of friends every widow deserves to have: they were available at any hour of the day or night, did not mind that I asked the same questions again and again from different angles, guided me through sorrow, distracted me creatively, and helped me to help others—which is always the best way through our own sorrow. Still, with so few resources available, learning Lenormand was hard.

One evening, after a long day of teaching and with my daughter at a play rehearsal, I sat on my big bed, where I still slept only on my side because the idea of having the whole thing to myself was still as untenable as it was factual, and I laid out a Grand Tableau for the month ahead. I had learned the archetypal meanings of each card, the card numbers, the lines and the boxes, and the chaining and the counting. Friends had started seeking me out for readings, and I had become something of a fixture in the online card community. Still, as I sat staring at that Grand Tableau, tired and a little overwhelmed by the cards that started swimming in front of my eyes because they had filled with tears, I heard a voice say my name.

I heard this voice in my right ear, which shocked me, as I have been completely deaf in that ear since infancy. Not only that, the voice I heard was my husband's, and, of course, he was not there. The third thing that took me aback were the words I heard him say in my deaf ear:

Erika, it's not childbirth.

After the shock of hearing his voice in an ear I do not hear out of, my snarky side sidled in, and I thought: "What does he know about childbirth, man that he is? Man that he *was*," I reminded myself. He was gone, after all. I felt again the pull toward sadness, but I felt a greater pull toward curiosity. My husband had said that it was *not* childbirth. That led me to first think about what childbirth *is*. In my experience, it was hard, painful, all-consuming. It required, it occurred to me, the pulling in of breath followed by a bearing down. Granted, I had missed that particular part of childbirth, having had an emergency C-section, but still . . . I felt that the bearing down part was what my husband was trying to tell me that card reading was *not*. But, I wondered, if reading cards did not require a bearing down, as my husband was insisting, what then, might be the opposite effort required?

In an instant, it came to me that the opposite of bearing down was . . . letting go. And I knew that letting go meant a letting go of ego and doubt, and a willingness to let Spirit rather than ego be my partner in this work. As soon as this realization washed over me, a lightness did too. Not only did the Grand Tableau laid out on my bed become completely clear, but I realized that, because I had already done the bearing down—the learning of Lenormand rules—I could let my inner Emily Dickinson take over and allow the words of Lenormand to arrange themselves in ways that were lovely and lyrical and my own, unorthodox as my approach to the Lenormand language might become.

I decided to create my own stripped-down Grand Tableau, a spread that would incorporate fewer than the full thirty-six cards, but enough to tell a satisfying story. I thought that if the Grand Tableau is a spread that says a little about a lot of things, what if I were to devise a spread that says a huge amount about a single issue? So that is what I created. I did not name the spread, but it is the spread I almost exclusively turn to when I read for anyone, and it has come to be known as Erika's Reading. Here it is:

Remember that any card in the Lenormand deck can serve as a significator? Recall the basic five-card spread I taught you in the beginning of this book? Erika's Reading is based on these two things, together with the fact that Lenormand is a word language with a grammar structure. Here are the steps to follow:

1. Decide on the issue on which you intend to read and which card you will use to represent that issue: Fish (34) = Money, Tree (5) = Health, Heart (24) = Love, etc. That card will be your significator.

2. Keeping that card in the deck, shuffle your cards using your preferred method, until you feel the deck is ready to speak to you.

3. With the cards face down and in your left hand, turn over each card one at a time with your right hand, until you arrive at your designated significator. Place that card in the center of your reading surface.

4. You now have two piles of cards: the ones you have already turned over and the ones in your left hand, which are still face down. From the turned-over pile on the right, take the top two cards and place them to the left of your significator. From the cards remaining in your left hand, turn over the top two, placing them to the right of your significator. You have just laid out a traditional Lenormand Line of Five. Now for the grammar part.

5. Put all of the remaining cards together into one pile face down. (There will be thirty-one cards, because five cards are already on the table.) Do not reshuffle yet.

6. Holding the thirty-one cards in your left hand, in a thoughtful, meditative way feel for what card in the deck you want to pull, and then place it just under the first card on the left in your Line of Five. Pull two more cards this same way and place them underneath the first one.

7. Working your way across the Line of Five, continue to feel for three cards to lay underneath each of the remaining cards, so that when you are done, you have a neat-looking box of twenty cards, with five across and four down.

8. Lastly, and because we always want to know more, pull a final three cards and lay them off to the side in the order you pulled them. The spread you pulled will look like this, the cards being numbered in the order in which they should be pulled:

2	3	1	4	5			
6	9	12	15	18			
7	10	13	16	19	21	22	23
8	11	14	17	20			

9. Card #1 is the card you will have preselected as significator. That top horizontal line (2, 3, 1, 4, 5) will give you an overview/summary of what you will see fully fleshed out in the body of the reading, so read that Line of Five in that way. It is the only line you will read horizontally until you get to the end of the spread.

10. Next, we read the vertical lines, starting with the one all the way to the left (2, 6, 7, 8). That line will give some backstory about the issue, and the information the line provides should prove familiar to the sitter. Broadly speaking, we can call this first vertical line the past.

11. The second vertical line (3, 9, 10, 11) is also backstory, past, but moves us forward a bit in terms of chronology. Sometimes, this line and the previous line are more aspirational than actual, but

both of these first two vertical lines identify the previous events and the hope and intention of the sitter. Sometimes these lines can also identify forces that have, to date, held the sitter back from forward movement. Context is everything.

12. The center line is the one you will read next (1, 12, 13, 14). This is the line that has at the top the card you chose as your significator, and it provides detail about what is going on right in the moment, in terms of both the events at play and the state of mind of your sitter. We can call this line the present.

13. The line directly to the right of that center line (4, 15, 16, 17) as well as the fifth and final vertical line (5, 18, 19, 20) provide information about outcome as well as advice. If you want to call these two lines the future, that would work.

14. Finally, we have the cards 21, 22, 23 off to the side. When I devised this spread, I thought back to when my daughter was very small and sat in my lap as I read her storybooks. I always let her select three before bedtime, and she always picked the longest books she could find. At the end of the last book, I would dramatically draw out the last two words in the book: *The End*, so that my daughter got the message that bedtime was at hand. Invariably, however, she would pull her thumb from her mouth and squirm around to face me. Always, her question was the same, "And *then* what happened?" Of course, at that point, all I wanted to do was put her in her crib and say good night, but instead, recognizing a teachable moment when I saw one, I would always answer her this way:

"What a great question! What do you think happens next?"

She would regale me with a sentence or two about what she thought the characters in the story might have said or done once the book was closed and the curtain had fallen, and always her theories were fun and funny and entirely plausible—all of which I told her. Only then would her eyelids sink to half-mast, indicating she was ready for sleep.

When I created my spread, the twenty-card box had a satisfying symmetry, but I found myself asking that same question of the cards as my daughter used to ask of me: "*Then* what happened?"

And because the whole point of the spread was not to recreate another Grand Tableau, I decided I would draw more cards, but only three. I call these cards the postscript, and they sometimes serve as confirmation of what the rest of the reading showed, while at other times, they act as a caveat. It is as though the cards want to say, "All of this is true, but remember this . . ." I hold my breath every time I draw the postscript, but always it is helpful and satisfying and makes me know that the cards have told me all they have to say on the subject for the moment. It is my reader's way of saying *The End*

• • •

On the following pages I've provided a sample Erika's Reading for you to play with on you own. I will choose as my significator the Book (26). Usually, this card refers to some mystery yet to be uncovered, but I am charging it to mean *this* book I am writing for you right now. How will those wanting to learn Lenormand feel about it? Have fun interpreting this!

The Cards

Dog (18) / Bouquet (9) / Book (26) / Ship (3) / Fish (34)

Child (13) / Whip (11) / Stork (17) / Birds (12) / House (4)

Clover (2) / Crossroads (22) / Anchor (35) / Tree (5) / Letter (27)

Mice (23) / Bear (15) / Ring (25) / Mountain (21) / Lily (30)

Postscript: Man (28) / Clouds (6) / Sun (31)

_____

_____

_____

_____

_____

_____

_____

_____

_____

_____

_____

_____

_____

The Layout

Postscript:

CHAPTER 21

Bonus Spreads

When I thought about adding some other short, nontraditional spreads for you to practice with, I had a couple of my own in mind, and I will add those here. However, my first thought was to reach out to one of my earliest, kindest, and best Lenormand teachers to see if she would give me permission to use one of her spreads, which I think is brilliant for its accuracy and simplicity and for the way in which it incorporates the use of Lenormand Houses to the absolute best advantage.

YES/NO

I have met many great Lenormandists in my years studying this instrument. Donnaleigh de la Rose and her YouTube channel Tarot Tribe beyond Worlds were invaluable resources for me when I first began learning Lenormand. In fact, there is a video on her channel that taught me to memorize all thirty-six cards and their numbers in about an hour, so I recommend you check her out. Donnaleigh has a six-card Lenormand spread she simply calls the Yes/No, which she is graciously allowing me to share here with you.

Many sitters come to readers wanting a simple yes or no to a burning question. As you can imagine, however, if you were to simply give them the yes or no, they would justifiably leave feeling unsatisfied, unfed. A good reader will want to do all they can to bring light and comfort to their sitter. Donnaleigh de la Rose's Six-Card Yes/No is perfect for this purpose.

1. Having been given your sitter's question, draw three cards and lay them in a horizontal line. These cards will serve as Houses. Remember that I taught you that every Lenormand card has a House as its native home. So, for example, if we were to take Ship (3), its House is in position three if the cards were to be laid out in order. But what does it mean for the Ship (3) to be in its House? Think of what a Ship (3) means: movement, travel, progress. Those are the qualities found in that House. What would happen, then, if in a reading, the Anchor (35) appeared in the House of the Ship (3)? Anchors are as nautical as ships are, of course, but Anchor (35) in the House of Ship (3) could well mean that no movement is possible, because the Anchor (35) weighs down any possible motion. What about if the Bouquet (9) appeared in a reading in the 9th House, which is its own? Would that not be an indication of blessings upon blessings?

2. Having laid out the three cards that will stand for Houses, your next step is to pull three more cards, placing one above each of the three previously pulled House cards. These three cards you should consider to be inhabiting the Houses of the previous three cards.

3. The mantra I always use when I read this spread is: Card A is in House X / Card B is in House Y / Card C is in House Z. That helps me focus. I don't use ABCs of course. Rather, I name the cards. You will get an immediate sense of whether you are looking at a yes or a no, but you also will get some detail, which is what your sitter will appreciate.

Example: a sitter asks me if their boyfriend will propose to them in the coming year, and I draw cards that look like this on the table, laying out the cards in the "houses" positions first:

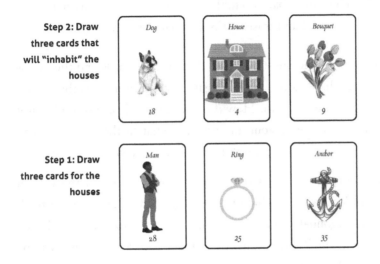

Step 2: Draw three cards that will "inhabit" the houses

Dog — 18
House — 4
Bouquet — 9

Step 1: Draw three cards for the houses

Man — 28
Ring — 25
Anchor — 35

Dog (18) / House (4) / Bouquet (9)

Man (28) / Ring (25) / Anchor (35) (These are the Houses.)

I would say: Dog (18) is in the House of the Man (28). House (4) is in the House of the Ring (25). Bouquet (9) is in the House of the Anchor (35). This looks like a yes, first of all. There is no Snake (7) or Cross (36) or Coffin (8) or Clouds (6), for example. But I can see more:

1. With Dog (18) in the House of the Man (28), this person is very loyal to the sitter, and his word is his bond.

2. With House (4) in the House of the Ring (25), this person is wanting to make a commitment to this sitter and create a life with her.

3. With Bouquet (9) in the House of the Anchor (35), the Anchor (35) takes on its most positive meaning, which is stability and safety, thanks to that Bouquet (9).

4.   Finally, mirror the card in the upper left corner with the card in the bottom right corner for any final piece of information. For example, in this spread, Dog (18) would be mirrored with Anchor (35). This combination emphasizes the fact that this person is, indeed, a loyal and trustworthy companion for this sitter.

5.   Using the same question, draw three House cards and then draw another three cards which will sit in those Houses. Is the answer you get a yes or a no? How do you know? How did the Houses help you arrive at your answer, and what further guidance can they provide to your sitter? Try this with any Yes/No question.

This spread is a great one to help you understand the role of Houses in Lenormand, which will assist you in Grand Tableau readings. What Donnaleigh did that is innovative is to take the Houses out of the Grand Tableau setting and make the case that they can be used in smaller spreads to great advantage.

EMILY'S SPREAD

Here is a small nine-card spread I devised myself, in honor of the poet Emily Dickinson during a visit to her hometown in the middle of writing this book. I wanted to give her a nod in this way because she was a poet who understood all the conventions of grammar, yet chose to deviate from those conventions for the sake of artistry. I know the rules of Lenormand. But in order to take my husband's otherworldly advice and let go instead of bearing down, I read and teach Lenormand my own unconventional way. Emily's Spread is my show of appreciation to her devotion to letting go. She has set us all a fine example. In keeping with the idea of letting go, I will simply show you the spread and leave you to your own devices:

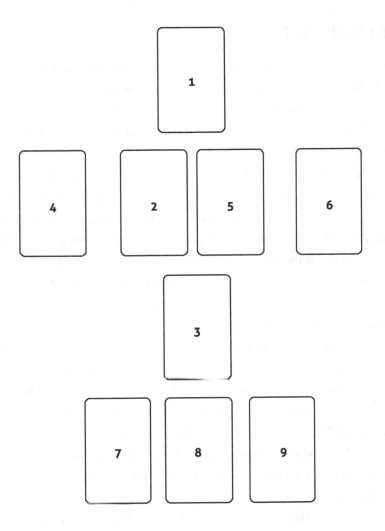

- Cards 1, 2, 3 lay out the situation in question.

- Cards 4, 5, 6 propose action to address the situation. Note that card 2 and card 5 are the same card.

- Cards 7, 8, 9 predict the outcome, should the proposed action be taken.

KEY SPREAD

Finally, here is a spread I devised meant to be reminiscent of the shape of a Key (33). As I mentioned in my earlier treatment of it, I consider this card to be the fraternal twin of the Sun (31). This spread speaks to the power of manifestation and the importance of personal agency and autonomy.

When we think of a key, we realize that there are, in effect, three parts to this little tool: There is the part we hold in our hands, which is the widest part. Then there is the long shaft of the key, the part we stick into the lock. Finally there is the tip of the key, which trips the mechanism on the lock such that the door we are seeking to unlock opens for us. In cards, the shape would be something like the layout shown on the facing page, with the bottom of the spread being that widest part we hold in our fingers.

As you see, this spread is read from the bottom to the top. In every moment, one has the opportunity to consider what thought one would most like to turn into a thing. At every point, should one of the cards or one of the questions the cards pose create doubt, be unanswerable, or seem irrelevant, then perhaps rather than proceeding with the reading the wiser thing would be to go back to the first question and ask yourself if this is really indeed the thing you want to manifest.

If, in fact, the cards that are on the table do answer the questions to your satisfaction, then you would proceed up the key's "ladder." Notice that the final two cards, in positions 7 and 8, are drawn face down, and you will turn over only one of those two cards to discover what the outcome of your manifestation will be. As there are, to paraphrase Robert Frost, some roads not taken, the card you do not turn over is the outcome that will remain a mystery. Personal agency requires choice, right? So make a selection, and then watch this thing grow from this thought.

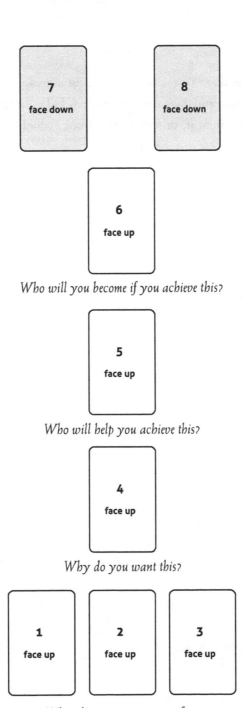

Who will you become if you achieve this?

Who will help you achieve this?

Why do you want this?

What do you want to manifest?

• • •

This book has done that: gone from being a dream of being able to learn such a powerful divination instrument as Lenormand, to healing with it and teaching it, to writing this book, which I hope will have breath and being far beyond myself.

Final Thoughts

I hope that this new way of learning to read brings you the same joy that picture books may have brought you as a child. I hope that once you learn the rules of the Lenormand language, you will make this healing instrument your own. I hope Lenormand does for you what it has done for me: brings you peace in times of pain, confidence in times of confusion, and mostly, works as an instrument that convinces you every time you hold the deck, you yourself are held and supported and known and loved by a Universe that, at every turn, is eager to help us transform thought into thing. And may all that you think to bring into being through the reading of the cards bring each of us and all of us into a more and more perfect union with ourselves and with each other. Let that be Lenormand's legacy.

ABOUT THE AUTHOR

Erika Robinson, an African-American Lenormandist, is an award-winning blogger. She speaks on and teaches Lenormand at conferences and online, both domestically and internationally. Erika has contributed to *The Cartomancer Magazine* as well as other publications. A graduate of Harvard University, Robinson has a bachelor's in English and a masters of divinity degree. Formerly a college admissions officer at Columbia and Princeton Universities, Robinson taught English in the New Jersey public school system for thirty years. She brings her love of language to all her work, including this book. Robinson lives and writes in Southern California. Find her at *www.lenormandwitherika.com, erikalenormand.substack.com* and on Instagram @divine_withme.

TO OUR READERS

Weiser Books, an imprint of Red Wheel/Weiser, publishes books across the entire spectrum of occult, esoteric, speculative, and New Age subjects. Our mission is to publish quality books that will make a difference in people's lives without advocating any one particular path or field of study. We value the integrity, originality, and depth of knowledge of our authors.

Our readers are our most important resource, and we appreciate your input, suggestions, and ideas about what you would like to see published.

Visit our website at *www.redwheelweiser.com*, where you can learn about our upcoming books and free downloads, and also find links to sign up for our newsletter and exclusive offers.

You can also contact us at *info@rwwbooks.com* or at

Red Wheel/Weiser, LLC
65 Parker Street, Suite 7
Newburyport, MA 01950